THE
NAME

A Journey Through the
Names and Character
of GOD

STUART BELL

RIVER
PUBLISHING

River Publishing & Media Ltd
Barham Court
Teston
Maidstone
Kent
ME18 5BZ
United Kingdom

info@river-publishing.co.uk

ISBN 978-1-908393-10-4

Printed in the UK

Contents

Acknowledgements

The material in this book originally came from a series I preached at New Life Lincoln. During the series I made extensive use of material from Andrew Wilson's book, *Incomparable*. I found his book and insights very helpful and want to express my thanks.

I am again indebted to Tim Pettingale who believed in this project and encouraged me to put the messages into print.

Thanks are also expressed to the administrative staff at New Life Lincoln and particularly to my P.A. Sadie Hoare for her behind-the-scenes work on manuscripts.

Finally, thanks go to Alan Hoare (MTh), who has been alongside me for many years, for his hard work converting source material from spoken to written word. I would like to honour him for his high level of support and his love of the Word of God.

1
What's in a Name?

"Then Moses said to God, 'If I come to the people of Israel and say to them, "The God of your fathers has sent me to you," and they ask me, "What is his name?" what shall I say to them?' God said to Moses, 'I AM WHO I AM.' And he said, 'Say this to the people of Israel, "I AM has sent me to you."' God also said to Moses, 'Say this to the people of Israel, "The LORD, the God of your fathers, the God of Abraham, the God of Isaac, and the God of Jacob, has sent me to you." This is my name forever, and thus I am to be remembered throughout all generations.'"
(Exodus 3:15-17 ESV)

"God spoke to Moses and said to him, 'I am the LORD. I appeared to Abraham, to Isaac, and to Jacob, as God Almighty, but by my name the LORD I did not make myself known to them.'"
(Exodus 6:2-3 ESV)

Throughout the Bible we read that there are many different names attributed to God, describing different facets of His being, and one name – I AM – that is used above all the others to refer to God. But the fact is, as God said to Moses in the verse above, we simply cannot confine God to a name. He is far too great in Himself to be fully revealed and therefore He can never be fully described in human terms.

It may seem obvious to say, but it is important we understand that God is much more than His title. "God" is a title we have attributed to Him in an attempt to identify Him, but the title doesn't tell us much about the Person. When people use the title "God" they often do so in the same way they might talk about a "president". There are many presidents in the world, so which president are they talking about? If we use the phrase "the President", then people may understand we are talking about the US President. But there is still a need to qualify to whom exactly we are referring. Saying "President Obama" qualifies our use of the title and now we know who we're referring to.

Similarly, when people talk about God, they are generally referring more to the title than the Person. So Scripture reveals numbers of "names of God" through which we can learn more about His Person and discover what He is like and how He wants to interact with us.

As far as I can see, every language in the world has a name for God. Not every language has a word for everything (as we can tell when we hear incongruous words like "Facebook" being transplanted into otherwise foreign dialects), but every language does have a word or a name for God. But just as there are many presidents in the world, so in different nations and cultures there are many "gods" which people believe in. They range from the North American Indian's "Great Spirit in the sky" to Islam's "Allah" to Hinduism's "Bhagwan". Looking through the Old Testament and examining the history of God's dealings with His people, we find that people believed in all kinds of gods for all manner of things. There were weather gods, fertility gods, gods of the earth, gods of the sky, and so on.

In the Bible, the names of gods, such as the Philistine god Dagon or the Canaanite gods Molech and Baal, would invoke fear in the people through rituals demanding subjugation. In contrast, Scripture shows how the relationship between the Israelites and the God of the Old Testament carries within it promises of hope, blessing, fruitfulness and protection. Today, in a secular society brimming with the worship of sport, music, image and wealth, it is all the more important we align ourselves with the living God who is over all the earth and all the heavens and who offers freedom from fear and bondage. To know Him is to know Him by name. God has many different names and Scripture unfolds these names to us, so that when we understand what they mean, we get to know Him better and better. As you continue to read this book you will discover how the names of God describe different facets of His character and nature, drawing you deeper into an encounter with Him.

In reality, society is influenced less by the images of God from the Bible itself and much more by the image that humanity has of Him. Artists, poets and musicians over the centuries have used their craft to convey God in particular ways, often in styles and concepts fitting with the fashion of the day. It is likely then that when somebody says to you, "I don't believe in God", they probably have an image in their head of a man with a big white beard sitting on a cloud clutching a trident.

It can be a useful thing to respond to their statement by saying, "Well neither do I!" I do not believe in a God who is remote and distant; One who, after creating the heavens and the earth, then removed Himself from any dealings with it. The truth of God's closeness to His creation cries out on every page of Scripture. He is intimately involved with our world: ever present, ever loving, everlasting.

It is very difficult to describe God. He can't be boxed in to specific words and images, however beautiful they are, and He can't be compared to anyone or anything. Three times in the book of Isaiah, God asks the nation of Israel, "To whom will you compare me?" In Isaiah 40:18 it says, "To whom then will you liken God, or what likeness compare with him?" (See also Isaiah 40:25 and 46:5 ESV)

Comparison is a useful tool when there is something new to be discovered. For instance, if we want to explain what chicken tastes like to someone who has never tasted it, we may say, "It is like eating duck, but has a less strong flavour." If the person responds by saying that they have never eaten duck, we may try and compare chicken to lamb, but point out the differences in texture and colour as well as taste. Although comparisons to God are difficult, we need some frame of reference in order to understand something about what we need to know and communicate it to others.

When a person asks, "What is God really like?" the answer is that we only know in part, since God cannot be compared to anything else. We can make a start by offering ideas such as, "God is good" or "God is gracious" or "God is kind" or "God is loving", but in truth, this is only scratching the surface. The bottom line is that we only get to know God because He has made Himself known to us first. He is not sitting around waiting to be discovered by a few intrepid explorers. Our faith is a revealed faith. God lovingly and generously reveals the truth about Himself to a heart that acknowledges its need of Him. When we read the Scriptures we receive revelation after revelation of who God is from the things He says about Himself and by the things He has done.

A name establishes identity

If you are a parent and you remember that great day when your child was born, you will know that one of the first things you considered was what name would be given to your child. Perhaps, like many others, you read through a book of baby names for inspiration, learning the meanings and origins of different words. In today's culture, unfortunately, the meanings of different names have become less and less important to the degree that some parents, over the last few decades, have given their children pretty outlandish names that reflect the parents' lifestyle more than the child's unique character. As Christians, however, we often put more thought or even prayer into what we will name our children and rightly so. In the Bible, the naming of a child was taken very seriously indeed and very often the name would have prophetic significance.

As soon as we name our newborn child we begin to get a sense of the identity of the child, especially when the name begins to be spoken over him or her. It would sound odd to go into a room and announce, "This is baby and I am Dad!" People want a bit more information than that in order to connect emotionally with this tiny human being. The baby's name, paradoxically, both releases and captures its identity and gives the family and community around it a sense of who they are. Very quickly the baby becomes associated with its name and vice versa.

I want to encourage you as you are reading this to understand that although you might not personally like your own name, it is a good name for you. That your particular name has been given to you is, in heaven's sight, very significant. Remember, your name is known throughout heaven. God knows it and He knows you.

Our associations with particular names can have positive and negative effects on us based on our experiences and memories. Growing up, I remember feeling scared every time I heard the name Stephen. There is nothing intrinsically bad about that name, of course, but for me it triggered something unpleasant in my memory. At school I was in a class with a big boy called Stephen. For one reason or another he was often very unkind to me, which made me anxious and fearful. So whenever I heard the name "Stephen" my mind and emotions were flooded with negative thoughts. It was purely a reflex reaction; his name had become something much bigger than just one word as it was deeply rooted in my experience.

That is a negative example of a specific name from my own past, but if we hear a name such as "Mother Theresa", it instantly has an altogether more positive connotation. We think of a little lady with immense strength and compassion who devoted her life to alleviating the suffering of the world's poorest people. We know who Mother Theresa is by simply hearing her name.

It is not only through people's names that we gather information and understanding. Choosing a name for a church is extremely important because people will get a sense of it's vision and purpose when they hear it. For instance, when our people go into the schools in Lincoln and the name of our church, "New Life", comes up in conversation, we hope that people see we are not a bunch of bores! We are into life in all its newness! (Unlike a couple of churches my good friend Jeff Lucas has visited in the past – "Hardly Pentecostal Church" and "Boring Assemblies of God Church"!)

A name establishes relationship

I'm always nervous in rooms that are full of people I don't know. It takes a great deal of courage from me to break the ice and start a conversation. Ice-breakers are often used as a method of making people feel more at ease in unfamiliar surroundings, but I am not a great fan of them! In fact, my pet hate is being required to wear a sticker with my name on it, which invites people to read who I am rather than hear me speak my name. More often than not, I find a simple introduction of, "Hello, my name is…" is as good as anything else. That way, I am beginning to establish a relationship and it starts with a name. In a room full of strangers it is so easy to feel vulnerable and exposed, but introducing myself is the first step in saying, "I would like to get to know you." Author Andrew Wilson says that "names are indicators of intimacy."

When I moved to big school all those years ago, the teachers insisted on referring to me as "Bell" rather than "Stuart". I had grown accustomed to being called Stuart at little school, which had been a happy place for me. Now, all of a sudden I found myself propelled into a whole new world where the culture was radically different and life was far from cosy. The teachers were there to teach me, plain and simple.

They were not there to be my friend, and this was reinforced by the use of my surname whenever they addressed me. When I tell people my name now, of course I use my first name because I understand that it is a point of connection in establishing a new friendship. You will never hear me introduce myself as "Bell"! I am "Stuart" and then, for those who get closer to me, my name is "Stu".

Some time ago, I preached alongside a world-renowned preacher. He preached powerful sermons and it put me under incredible pressure because he was so good; everything he did was brilliant and everybody loved him. I know that we don't preach to impress people or to compete with one another, but in such a situation one inevitably feels the pressure to speak well and, hopefully, open up an opportunity for spiritual blessing and breakthrough. What I especially liked about this man was that after he had spoken and before I was due to preach, he was really friendly towards me. He started chatting to me and I thought to myself that this was really wonderful. Here was a speaker of world-renown and I was in the process of becoming his friend. Fantastic!

At the end of the conference and before we left to go, he told me he would love to give me one of his bestselling books. It seemed to me that our relationship was going from strength to strength. He then told me, "What's more, I've written a little something on the inside page of the book." I thought to myself that it couldn't get better than this: he was fast becoming one of my closest friends. Reading the kind words he had written I saw that he had addressed it, "Dear Steve…"! Since names establish a relationship, and despite the fact that we were attempting to become friends, I realised that we were not quite there yet!

The beauty of Christianity is that it is a relational faith. We have a Father God, we have an elder brother called Jesus, and our constant companion is called the Holy Spirit. We have been born again into a family and we find that we also have brothers and sisters in Christ who we grow to love. Many of us would say that we "know" God as our Father, but how many of us know Him really well? If we were to mark the depth of our relationship with Him out of ten, I wonder what we would honestly put down?

The reality is, if we really want to know God we must first acquaint ourselves with Jesus. It is through Jesus that we get to know the Father. I will deal with this more fully in subsequent chapters, but here is a reminder of what Jesus Himself said: "No one comes to the Father except through Me. If you had known Me, you would have known My Father also" (John.14:6-7 ESV).

A name reveals character

In the Bible, particularly in the Old Testament, when a name was given to someone it was normally to signify something very important about them. It either held significance about a situation that they were born into or spoke prophetically about the destiny ahead of them. Parents would often seek God before they gave their child his or her name, expecting Him to reveal something new. In the New Testament the account of the birth of John the Baptist includes the words God Himself spoke through the angel Gabriel to the parents about what to name the child. Zacharias was told to name his son "John". When the day came, there was a little controversy about it from those around, due to the fact that no one in the family had previously been given that name. Zacharias was firm, however, because he knew that this was God's chosen name for his son and that there was a significant destiny for this John who was going to become the forerunner of Christ (Luke 1:5-25).

Joseph, who married Mary – who was at that time carrying the unborn Christ-child – was explicitly commanded by the angel to call the infant "Jesus", a name meaning "saviour", which was emphasised by the angel who promised, "for he will save his people from their sins" (Matthew.1:21 ESV).

On occasion God changed people's names for different reasons. He renamed "Abram" as "Abraham" (Genesis 17:5). "Abram" means, "exalted father" and "Abraham" means "father of a multitude". God had a purpose for Abraham far greater than being the head of his household: he was to be a father of nations! In the renaming, God left room for Abraham to grow in character and stature as the true meaning of his destiny was made known.

Jacob's name literally means "twister". When God changed his name to "Israel", which means "prince or ruler with God", it clearly stated what God had in mind for his future (Genesis 32:27-28). The point at which God asked Jacob to say his own name – "...and what is your name?" (verse 27) – was a key event for Jacob as he was given an opportunity to describe himself as he really was at that moment. As he owned up to whom he really was in character, God was then able to change his name to something much more positive, giving a strong prophetic indication as to who he was to become. In this process, it was as if God was saying, "You have struggled and manipulated your way through life, but now you have wrestled for a blessing, I will cause you to become a prince and a ruler in harmony with God." It was a profound moment for Jacob.

In the New Testament, we have more examples of people's names being changed. In Matthew's gospel, Jesus first approaches Simon the fisherman and invites him on a journey (Matthew 4:18). The name "Simon" means "one who hears". This is intriguing because later in the gospel when Jesus asks the disciples to identify who He (Jesus) really is, the revelation comes to Simon.

"He said to them, 'But who do you say that I am?' Simon Peter replied,

'You are the Christ, the Son of the living God.' And Jesus answered him, 'Blessed are you, Simon Bar-Jonah! For flesh and blood has not revealed this to you, but my Father who is in heaven.'" (Matthew 16:15-17 ESV)

Simon heard something by revelation that was to bring about a name change for him. Instead of remaining "Simon" he was given the name "Peter", which means "rock". Effectively, Jesus was saying to him that on the rock of the revelation that Simon had just received, the strength of the Church would be built.

God has many names

So what about God's name? How does God's name reveal His character and encourage us in our relationship with Him? As I alluded to earlier in this chapter, God is not restricted to just one name, He has hundreds of them and we will be exploring the meaning of some of them in this book. God wants to reveal Himself to each one of us, day by day, in whatever stage of life we find ourselves. There is a name of God that applies to your particular situation today that will encourage, strengthen and comfort you. Over 6,800 times in the Old Testament alone, God is referred to by a particular name and each one of those names exists today, flowing through Him, revealing more and more about His identity, character and desire for relationship with His world.

To walk closely with God we are required to change into His likeness by opening ourselves to a loving relationship with Him that grows deeper and more intimate throughout our lives. In order to do that, it helps to know who He really is, because then we can trust ourselves to Him. In order to understand, we need to search the Scriptures and experience His presence day by day. He wants to meet with us, to show us the truth about His nature and character in all its multi-faceted glory. When God made himself known to Moses, He used these amazing words,

"The LORD, the LORD, a God merciful and gracious, slow to anger, and abounding in steadfast love and faithfulness, keeping steadfast love for thousands, forgiving iniquity and transgression and sin, but who will by no means clear the guilty, visiting the iniquity of the fathers on the children and the children's children, to the third and the fourth generation." (Exodus 34:6-7 ESV)

In the Hebrew language, the name that is usually used for "God" is actually four letters, four consonants and no vowels. The letters are "YHWH". This name is called a tetrogrammaton, which means "the word having four letters". It is translated in our English Bibles with the four capital letters "LORD". This name means "the eternal, self-existent One". But the English language does not really give us a meaningful impression of that name and we do not really know how the name of God was exactly pronounced in those days. Most scholars feel that the closest that we can get is to use the name "YAHWEH". Other scholars, writing from a more liberal point of view, favour the name "JEHOVAH".

Now what is the difficulty? We know we can say "God" as a title, but for the intimate knowledge of who God really is, we have to dig a little bit deeper. The Hebrew people, when they were referring to God, would be afraid to speak aloud His name. For them, the name of God was so sacred that they would not pronounce it for fear of bringing judgement on themselves. They held God's name in high esteem, reverence and honour, taking the commandment that forbade taking it in vain very seriously indeed (Exodus 20:7). Reverence for the name of God was extremely important and it still is. To the Jews, the name

"YHWH" remains sacred to this day.

The sanctity of God's name is actually something that Jesus Himself pointed out to His disciples and also to us who believe and pray. We need to come to that place of reverence in addressing of God. Jesus taught that when we pray, we should say, "Our Father, who art in heaven, hallowed be Your name" (Matthew 6:9-13). Did you notice the "Hallowed be your name" part? It is interesting that it is the Saxon English word "hallowed" that is used here. In fact, this word is only found twice in the whole Bible and both the occurrences are in the prayer framework that Jesus gave us. It is a translation of the Greek word Hagiazo which means, "to consecrate for sacred use". It is the same as saying, "Holy is your name" or "sacred is your name", but all translators have chosen to use the word "hallowed".

How do we "hallow" the name of God? First, by giving His name the respect and reverence that it deserves. The whole person of God is tied into His name, so to make light of the name is to make light of Him. It is also interesting to note that in the beginning of this prayer framework, Jesus encourages us to first of all use the name "Father". This would have been shocking to His Jewish audience, who would have been brought up on Names like Yahweh – "the eternal, self-existent One" or El Shaddai – "the all powerful One". This was like telling them that they could go into the presence of the One whose name was too sacred to even utter, the King of kings, and call him "Papa", a title of intimacy and love. The lesson is clear: appreciate the closeness and respect the greatness.

In our busy lives, it is easy to not take the time to think deeply about this aspect of God. He is so vast that it is impossible to compare this God of all the earth to any other god – there is no way it can be done. That is why it is so easy to become tongue tied when we try to adequately describe God to others.

I Am what I Am

Most likely the name "YAHWEH" is rooted in the passage found in Exodus 3:15-17. Moses had been given a huge task to accomplish – to bring the children of Israel out of captivity in Egypt. He had to go and address the great Pharaoh of the day asking him to let His people go. When Moses asks, "Who shall I say has sent me?" God, in response, brings a revelation to Moses of the most intimate kind, giving him a clue as to the meaning of His name and explaining why he has the right to speak to Pharaoh with such authority, commanding him to release the nation of Israel. He says to Moses, "I am who I am." This can also be translated "I am what I am" or "I will be what I will be". God continued, "Say this to the people of Israel, 'I AM has sent me to you.'" The word "Yahweh" and the Hebrew word "to be" sound very similar, so effectively, God is saying, "Tell them I AM has sent you."

Because God is greater than any other God, His name is greater than any other name. What is He saying here? He is saying this: "I will be what I will be". Actually, He is saying more than that: "I will be what you need me to be when you need me to be it." He is revealing His faithfulness, His love, His mercy, His protection and so much more. God simply says, "I AM".

Once we understand for ourselves that God, the eternal, self-existent One is with us, and that He will be Himself among us, then we can face any situation in life, whatever it may be, with confidence and courage.

At the end of each chapter in this book there will be time to reflect and pray. It is good to take time and let God reveal more of who He is through His different names. We all need to have a revelation, a moment of insight into His greatness, His love and His power. Time and time again in Scripture God bestows special names to those He loves, first to a nation called Israel and now to us. To both Jews and Gentiles who are in Christ that name becomes very precious, because it is a covenant relationship name, and it is to do with the very heart and character of God. Ultimately He has made Himself known in His son Jesus – another name we will look at later in this book. In Philippians 2:9-11, Paul tells us that God, "has highly exalted him, and bestowed on him the name that is above every other name, so that at the name of Jesus every knee should bow, in heaven and on earth and under the earth, and every tongue confess that Jesus Christ is Lord, to the glory of God the Father" (ESV). Jesus has a name that is higher than any other.

Andrew Wilson has written a book called Incomparable which has helped me in discovering this truth. He writes, "I am convinced that if your knowledge of God doesn't grow, then neither will you." If we want to grow and become more like Jesus, if we want to do more things that please Him, then we need to grow in the knowledge of who He is and we need to get to know Him more. He has revealed Himself to us as the great "I AM". He is telling us that He is at the beginning of all things and He is also at the end of all things. He is the "Alpha and the Omega" (Revelation 1:8).

If you put an A-Z together of the names of God, you would only scratch the surface with the following. He is…

… the Anointed, the Apostle, the Author, the Alpha, the Amen, the Ancient of Days, the Beginning, the Begotten, the Beloved, the Branch, the Bread, the Bridegroom, the Bright Morning Star, the Bishop of our souls, the Captain, the Consolation, the Chief Corner Stone, the Counsellor, the Covenant, the Christ, the Deliverer, the Daystar, the Door, the Dawn, the Desire of all nations, the Elect, the Everlasting, the Emmanuel, the Forerunner, the Friend, the First

Fruits, the Faithful God, the Fountain, and He is the Fisher of men. He is God. He is the Gift of God, the Grace, the Governor – He is in charge; He is our Guide, the Glory, the Glorious Lord, the Help, He is our Hope, our Husband, our Healer, our Hero, the Horn of Salvation, the Head of the Church. He is the Heir of all things. He is Hell's dread and Heaven's wonder. He is Holy and He's the great I AM. He is the Inheritance, the image of God's Person; He is Immortal, Invisible and Invincible. He is Judah, Just, Judge, Jesus. He is King of Israel, the King of Kings, the King of Glory, the King of Everlasting. He is Life! He is Love, the Lion, the Lamb, the Living Stone, the Lord of Glory, the Messenger, the Messiah, the Maker, our Mediator, our Master, our Mercy, the Mighty God, the Nazarene, the Offspring of David, the Only Begotten, the Omega, the Offering. He is our Priest, our Pastor, our Passover, our Prophet, our Prince of Peace. He is our Physician, our Rock, He is Righteous, the Rabbi, the Root of David, the Refiner, the Restorer, our Redeemer, our Refuge, the Resurrection, the Stone, our Shepherd, the Son of God, the Son of Man, the Servant, the Seed, our Saviour, the Sacrifice, He is the same yesterday, today and forever. He is our Teacher, He is the Truth, the Tree of Life, the Witness, the Word and the Way. He is our Wonderful Counsellor, the Wisdom of God. He is the Bright Morning Star and He is the Lover of your soul. He is the Way, He is the Truth and the Life. He is the Alpha and the Omega, the Beginning and the End. He is the Lord Jesus Christ. He is Yahweh, the King of Kings and the Lord of Lords; great and glorious is His Name!

Reflect and pray...

God knows me by name. I may or may not like the name I have been given, but that does not matter to God who speaks it with love when addressing me.

"Thank you, Lord, that while your names reveal your greatness and majesty, you are not remote and lofty, you are intimate and loving. Each one of your wonderful names speaks of the truth of who you are and what you can do. Thank you that I can apply any of your names to any situation I find myself in and, as I do, I will encounter your presence, finding joy, comfort, hope and encouragement on my life's journey. Amen."

2

The God Who is There

It is the manifest presence of God that marks out Christianity from all other faiths. Reading through the Old Testament we can see that there is revelation upon revelation about God and His interaction with His people. Into the New Testament, the birth, life, death and resurrection of Jesus shows us the lengths to which God was prepared to go to save and love His world. After the ascension, the coming of the Holy Spirit at Pentecost marks the permanent deposit and presence of God in power and from Genesis to Revelation, there is God: He is always there and nothing has changed. The guarantee of the Holy Spirit means that every day, as we walk through life, His presence remains with us. What a comfort!

Ezekiel: the puzzle and the promise

The Bible has a specific name for "The Lord who is there". In the very last verse of the book of Ezekiel we read this about the new city of God:

"The circumference of the city shall be 18,000 cubits. And the name of the city from that time on shall be The LORD is there." (Ezekiel 48:35 ESV)

The Hebrew phrase for "The Lord is there" is, YAHWEH SHÂMMAH. Not only is this the last sentence in the book of Ezekiel, but it is also the last revealed name in a sequence of revealed names throughout the Old Testament. YAHWEH SHÂMMAH – The LORD who is there.

It is true to say that Ezekiel is not an easy book to understand as it is both prophetic and apocalyptic. The word "apocalyptic" comes from the Greek word apokálypsis which literally means "the uncovering – the lifting of a veil". In other words, apocalyptic writings show us what is yet to come. It is not easy for people in the Western world to understand this kind of language. I referenced a number of commentaries to try and get some light on what is happening in the book of Ezekiel and I found one particular commentary by Stuart Briscoe, who had titled the whole book, "All things weird and wonderful" which gives us a rough idea of what Ezekiel is like!

Working our way through the book of Ezekiel we encounter visions of God, useless vines, rotten figs and eagles. We find whirling wheels, living creatures and wheels with rims full of eyes. There are briars and thorns, assorted scorpions and dry bones in valleys. Towards the end of the book there is a land without inhabitants, a city without citizens, a temple without priests and a ritual without worshippers. So not just weird and wonderful but perhaps also complex and confusing!

Near the end of the book Ezekiel is seeing the setting up of an ideal city, a city that is yet to come, and within it he sees a restored temple. In fact, if we go through a number of the closing chapters there is great deal of information regarding the setting up of that temple with all its details and dimensions. The only problem with it is that the temple he is describing has not yet been built.

What does this mean? What is the book of Ezekiel teaching us today? Is this envisioned temple yet to be built in Jerusalem? Is it a picture of the Church? Is it a vision of the final city of God?

It is so easy to become befuddled with the specifics contained in a book of the Bible written in this kind of prophetic and apocalyptic style. The best way to approach it is to study it in order to apply it to everyday life. In fact, all theology must always be earthed in practical ways. I could try to answer all the questions one might have about Ezekiel in the following pages, but that is not the task of this book. The key issue to know is that after all of the visions, pictures, enigmatic puzzles and prophecies found in Ezekiel's prophecies, there is a comforting revelation contained right at the end of the book. Ezekiel says that whatever is going to happen in the future, whatever is going to happen with temples and cities, whatever is going to happen with regard to the rule of God in the days that are ahead, a specific revelation of the name of God will sustain all things. That name is "YAHWEH SHÂMMAH – The Lord who is there.

There are a number of people who believe they have the future worked out. They know exactly what is going to take place, they know exactly when Jesus is going to return (which, incidentally, is a lot more than Jesus knew when He was on the earth!), they know all about where the great tribulation fits and they have a good understanding of the post-, pre- and a-millennial eschatological positions. I am not too clued up on some of these theological positions, but one thing I do know is this: whatever happens tomorrow and in the days that are ahead, wherever we are, the Lord is there and that is good enough for me.

Ours is a faith in which God is always present. Just pause for a moment and let the truth of this sink in. The God who is from the beginning, who formed the earth has expressed a desire to be present with His people always. His presence with men, women and children reflects the relationship between the Godhead – Father, Son and Holy Spirit. Too often religion is all about men and women striving to be good enough to reach God. Authentic relationship with God, on the other hand, flows from His quest to reach out to us in order to presence Himself with us. Although we may not understand exactly what the future will bring, one thing we do know is that God has it all in His hands. He is at the beginning and He is also at the end.

He is there when we least expect it

In Genesis chapter 28, Jacob embarks on a journey out of Canaan to find a wife. Reaching the land of Haran and seeing that the sun has begun to set, he decides to settle down for the night. Taking one of the stones for a pillow, he lies down, much wearied from his journey and is soon asleep.

"And he came to a certain place, and stayed there that night because the sun had set." (Genesis 28:11 ESV)

As far as Jacob was concerned, the place he came to rest was just an ordinary place, a desert place with nothing remotely special about it. However, that place became "a certain place" where his destiny would be marked out and where he would experience the presence of God.

Many of us can identify with this. We wake up one morning thinking that it is going to be an ordinary day, but it becomes a day of destiny where God visits us by His presence quite unexpectedly. It may happen during a chance conversation, a walk in the country, in church, in the supermarket or at the office. Whatever way it takes place, it interrupts our day and an encounter with the God who is there, changes the shape of our lives.

For Jacob, this happened to him as he slept and came in the form of a vivid and unusual dream in which he saw a stairway or ladder resting on the earth with its top reaching up into heaven. He saw angels of God ascending and descending upon it, signifying a divine interaction between heaven and the earth. I believe that Jacob, whilst he was dreaming, understood that he was experiencing a revelation from God of His purposes for mankind. As he saw the Lord standing above the ladder, God then said to him, "I am the Lord, the God of your father Abraham and the God of Isaac" (Genesis 28:13 ESV). God revealed Himself quite unexpectedly to Jacob who then found himself in the very presence of God. It is clear that Jacob knew the dream was from God because when he woke up the substance of that dream was still living within him.

"Then Jacob awoke from his sleep and said, "Surely the Lord is in this place, and I did not know it." And he was afraid and said, "How awesome is this place! This is none other than the house of God, and this is the gate of heaven." (Genesis 28:16-17 ESV)

God was with Jacob, revealing Himself as YAHWEH SHÂMMAH – The Lord who is there.

I sleep quite well and dream a lot, especially if I have eaten pizza for tea! Sometimes I dream I am being chased; other times I am trying to run but my legs are rooted to the spot and I am unable to move. These are common dreams and many people I know have identical ones.

There have been two occasions in my life when I would say that I have really had a "God-dream". I knew they were special because they were so different from all the others. They were in full Technicolor, to begin with, and accompanied by all kinds of different sounds, and to this day I remember them in fine detail. Due to the personal nature of the content of the dreams, I can't elaborate too much, but I will say that what God revealed to me in them came to pass in the most amazing ways.

Here, in the Western world, we are not too open to God speaking to us in dreams and we tend to label people who claim to have messages from God in their dreams as a little eccentric. In the Middle East, however, there is a greater openness to this kind of heavenly communication and there are many reports that God has often spoken to people through dreams.

The story of Jacob's dream in Genesis chapter 28 helps us to understand that God can be there when we least expect it. God's presence is not just reserved for church meetings! His name YAHWEH SHÂMMAH reassures us that He is ever-present, wherever we go and whatever we do. Whether we are in a desert wilderness or in a fruitful place, God is there with us and will reveal Himself to us in exactly the ways we need Him to. We can be in an unexpected place and He can come to us at an unexpected time. The Psalmist actually tells us that we can never get away from the presence of God. David wrote in Psalm139:7-10,

"Where shall I go from your Spirit? Or where shall I flee from Your presence? If I ascend to heaven, You are there! If I make my bed in Sheol, You are there! If I take the wings of the morning and dwell in the uttermost parts of the sea, even there Your hand shall lead me, and Your right hand shall hold me." (ESV)

He is there when we are tested in the fires of life

Let me take you to a second familiar story that we find in the third chapter of the book of Daniel. The background to this book is that the people of God had been taken into captivity. No longer in Jerusalem, they were now exiled to Babylon. Within the group of young men who had been taken, there were some who were determined that they would follow the Lord in a foreign land and culture, whatever the cost.

In Babylon they were faced with many challenges: a different language, a different way of thinking, a different diet and different expectations. It is no different in our 21st century world. We are citizens of heaven and we live in a world that has very different values and lifestyles. We need to take inspiration from Daniel and his friends. We need to know how to be followers of God in an alien culture.

God was with Daniel and his friends as they took a stand against being forced to eat the King's diet. As they respectfully reasoned with their overseer, God gave them favour (see Daniel 1:1-16).

Later, King Nebuchadnezzar decided to construct a large statue of gold in honour of himself and commanded all the people to fall down and worship it at the given signal. Failure to do so would result in an immediate death sentence. Shadrach, Meshach and Abednego, the three friends of Daniel, refused to comply with the king's orders, declaring that they would only bow the knee to the one true God – YAHWEH. I have to ask myself what I would do under a similar set of circumstances. I might pray, "Lord, although I am physically bowing down and complying with this edict on the outside, you know that on the inside, I am really still standing to honour you. I know that you can see my heart – that I am frightened of the prospects of the flame and yet I don't want to dishonour you – so I am half-bowing, hoping that no one but you will notice!"

But these three friends were resolute in their decision, stating that they could not obey the king's edict and that they would trust the Lord to deliver them. Furthermore, even if the Lord did not deliver them, they said they would still not bow down to the king's statue. To be honest, this is the kind of calibre that is so desperately needed in our land today. There is a need for men and women who are so resolute in their commitment to Christ that they will risk everything for the honour of His name. Nebuchadnezzar was so angered by their stand that he commanded the heat of furnace to be increased to be seven times hotter than normal. He then had them thrown into it, killing the guards in the process.

When the men entered the furnace, something wonderful took place. The Bible tells us that King Nebuchadnezzar leapt to his feet in utter astonishment when he suddenly saw four men, not three, walking around unharmed in the flames. He responded by calling his counsellors to him, asking them the exact number of men that had been thrown in the furnace. They quickly confirmed that only the three friends had been thrown in. Nebuchadnezzar is brought abruptly to his senses, humbled by the incredible manifestation of God's presence in the furnace with Shadrach, Meshach and Abednego. The fourth man was, in his own words, "like the son of the gods" (Daniel 3:25 ESV). Bible commentators would say that this was a "theophany" – a pre-incarnation manifestation of Christ. He was there with them right in the middle of the furnace. YAHWEH SHÂMMAH – The Lord who is there.

There are lots of mysteries to be found in this story, not least why God would allow them to be thrown in the fire in the first place. What is most important, however, is that while in the fire they didn't get burned as they were joined by a divine presence: God Himself was there with them in the fire, in their severe time of testing.

I remember visiting my old friend Rich Hubbard with my son Dave. At the time, Rich was suffering from a rare and virulent form of cancer and as we drove down, just to pray for him, we knew he was seriously ill. When we arrived, we asked him whether the Lord was saying anything to him by way of encouragement and blessing. He responded by saying that the Lord had spoken to him about this very scenario of the three friends in the furnace. His testimony to us, and to all around him, was, God can deliver me, but even if he chooses not to, then I am still totally committed to being a follower of the Lord Jesus Christ. That is a real and authentic faith and we know that while Rich was not delivered from the disease and went to be with Jesus, he was resolute in his love, hope and commitment to his Lord to the end. This was the testimony of his life.

It is well known that being under pressure creates stress and we can experience all kinds of odd physical and emotional symptoms. But it is also clear that many people experience an unusual and wonderful grace that comes upon them during difficult times. It is evidence of the close presence of God who is there in every test and fire that we go through. He does not abandon us and leave us to perish under the fiery onslaughts. The writer to the Hebrews reminded the beleaguered Christians in the 1st Century that Jesus had said, "I will never leave you nor forsake you" (Hebrews13:5 ESV).

In the Old Testament, God spoke to the Hebrew nation through the prophet with these words: "When you pass through the waters, I will be with you; and through the rivers, they shall not overwhelm you; when you walk through fire you shall not be burned, and the flame shall not consume you" (Isaiah 43:2 ESV). He is there when we least expect it. He is there when we are tested in the fires of life.

He is there when the shadows fall upon our lives

I want to take you to the well known 23rd Psalm. This is the Psalm that we read so often at funerals and times of bereavement because it brings us comfort and blessing. We remember the verse that says, "Even though I walk through the valley of the shadow of death I will fear no evil for You are with me" (Psalm 23:4 ESV). We see again YAHWEH SHÂMMAH – The Lord who is there. David continues by saying in the same verse that, "Your rod and your staff they comfort me."

The presence of God comes to us in a very special way when the shadows fall.

When we carefully examine the grammar of this psalm, we see that from the outset David is speaking about the LORD. He writes, "The Lord is my shepherd; I shall not want. He makes me lie down in green pastures. He leads me beside still waters. He restores my soul. He leads me in paths of righteousness for his name's sake" (v1-3). He then goes on to write about the valley of the shadow of death and we will see that the grammar changes from speaking about the Lord to speaking to the Lord: "Even though I walk through the valley of the shadow of death I will fear no evil for **you are** with me." Why the change in grammar? Is it not possible that when David recalled the valley times of his life, he also recalled the nearness of God and instinctively began talking to Him rather than writing about Him?

In Psalm 46:1 we read that in times of trouble God is a "very present help". Before the word "present" we see the word "very". God is "very present".

This particular phrase is only ever found here in the Bible. In the original Hebrew language it is expressed forcefully – the word "very" is the word "meod" which literally means "vehement" or "severe". It can therefore be said that God is "vehemently present" with us, or more colloquially, He is "in our face" in times of trouble. He is a lot closer than we think.

This verse also tells us that He is found in a time of trouble. It could be easy to assume that as He is called the Prince of Peace, He draws closest to us in a time of peace or blessing. But the reality is that it is often in the darker moments of our lives that He is the most real. The Greek version of the Old Testament (LXX) puts it like this: He is "a help in the afflictions that come heavily upon us." Someone once said, "I would rather walk in the valley with God than on the mountaintop without Him."

Shadows only occur because somewhere there is a light. In total darkness there are no shadows. The Bible teaches us that Jesus is the light of this world and because of that, if there is a shadow there is most certainly the presence of the Lord. Whatever people have to go through, whether it is a hard valley experience or the pain of bereavement, God is there.

Miss White

There was a time when I had never taken a funeral, never seen anyone die, and had never been with a dying person. I remember clearly when, as a young pastor, all that changed. It was when I was out taking a youth meeting one night about 20 miles away from my home that the telephone rang. On the other end was the sister of a lady called Miss White, who informed me that Miss White had asked her to contact me. The sister told me that Miss White believed she was going to die that very night and she wanted to know if I could come and be with her when it happened.

I must say that I did feel a little bit vulnerable at this point. It was completely outside of my comfort zone and I was in unfamiliar territory. But I knew I wanted to go and that I would do my very best for her. I left the meeting where I was speaking and drove to her house, all the time thinking to myself that I had not been in a situation like this before and I wondered how I would handle it. I decided that as I am a pastor, a shepherd, I needed to do what shepherds do. Shepherds care, shepherds read the Word of God to their flock, shepherds bring hope, shepherds talk about God's goodness and they point to the fact that death is not the end. So I decided that I would read Scripture to her and pray with her as she died.

When I arrived, I was welcomed into the bungalow and the sister took me into the room where Miss White was lying on her bed. She was in considerable pain and almost unconscious. I sat at her side in a chair and started to read the Scriptures to her, trying to remember all of the verses that would be applicable to the situation! I read from John's gospel about many mansions and I also read some passages about the hope that is to come – the hope of the resurrection.

It was when I came to read the Psalms that the atmosphere in the room changed. I started with Psalm 20 then went to Psalm 23, speaking these words over her: "Even though I walk through the valley of the shadow of death I will fear no evil for you are with me, your rod and staff they comfort me." In that little room on that particular day, I had a real sense that YAHWEH SHÂMMAH was there. I read her several psalms that evening and eventually came to Psalm 91, a very special Psalm. I began to speak it over her and then I came to the verse, "For He will give His angels charge concerning you" (Psalm 91:11 NASB). As the words left my mouth I could feel the warmth of the presence of God in the room. All of a sudden, Miss White sat up in bed and she said, "Angels are here!" As she said this, I became very quiet and I simply sat there in this holy stillness.

The next words that came out of her mouth I will never forget. She looked at me and said, "Well, I'm not going to die. I'll make you a cup of tea, duck!" And that is exactly what she did. She got out of bed, put the kettle on and said again, "It's alright, duck, I'm not going to die!" In my astonishment, all I could say was, "Well, thank the Lord!" I wasn't really prepared for this. The pain in her body had vanished and she was healed at that moment when heaven came into the room.

The story is a fascinating one. I don't understand all the ways of God and I don't need to, because there must always be the element of mystery in our faith. What I do know is that exactly a year to the day and to the time, when Miss White was in her kitchen, she suddenly dropped down dead and went to be with the Lord. I thank the Lord for Miss White!

Do you know He is there as the shadows fall?

My wife Irene and I love the magic of Christmas. A few years ago we had been to the Christmas Eve service at the church and we were just getting ready to go to bed around midnight when the telephone rang. We know that when we receive calls after midnight, it is not usually a good thing. So it was that we heard that Irene's father had been rushed into hospital and we found ourselves for a good part of the night and

Christmas Day sitting in a hospital ward with a very ill Lionel, the magic and the atmosphere of Christmas quickly evaporating before our eyes.

We tried to make sense of it all, asking ourselves why this should happen on one of our favourite times of the year. We wrestled with both feelings of sadness and feelings of frustration that our family Christmas celebration was being robbed with Irene's father being so ill. As we struggled, we found a place of peace as we realized that there was a bigger dimension at work, exerting an influence. The Lord was there. Lionel never came out of hospital, but the truth of the matter was that the presence of the Lord was with us throughout the time when the shadow of death fell over our lives.

The Lord is there when we face the issues of bereavement and death. Unfortunately, we live in such a materialistic world that we quickly lose sight of the reality of heaven. For a Christian to draw his last breath and go into the presence of the Lord is a wonderful thing. The Bible says, "Precious in the sight of the Lord is the death of his saints" (Psalm 116:15 ESV). During a conversation with an experienced nurse some years ago, she said to me, "You know, when an unbeliever dies, you can sense a spirit of death that has come. On the other hand, when a Christian dies, you know that it is Jesus who comes Himself to their deathbed." The Lord is there when the shadows fall.

He is there in the Incarnation

The word "incarnation" is the word that we use to explain the theology of the eternal God taking on human form and becoming a man. It is one of the greatest miracles that we could ever imagine. Paul the apostle encapsulates it for us in his letter to the Philippians:

"...Christ Jesus, who, though He was in the form of God, did not count equality with God a thing to be grasped, but made Himself nothing, taking the form of a servant, being born in the likeness of men. And being found in human form, He humbled himself by becoming obedient to the point of death, even death on a cross." (Philippians 2:5-8 ESV)

God, the eternal Creator of all became man, taking on the form of a baby. The Son of God became incarnate, birthed into the obscure regions of the Middle East over 2000 years ago and ancient prophecies given to Israel found their fulfilment in it. God came down to where we were. God spoke through the prophet Isaiah, saying, "Therefore the Lord himself will give you a sign. Behold, the virgin shall conceive and bear a son, and shall call his name Immanuel" (Isaiah 7:14 ESV). The name Immanuel means, "God with us". YAHWEH SHÂMMAH – The Lord who is there. Charles Wesley put it so eloquently when he penned these words: "Let earth and Heaven combine, Angels and men agree, to praise in songs divine the incarnate Deity, Our God contracted to a span, incomprehensibly made Man."

This is the real reason why we celebrate Christmas. On that wonderful day, the angels celebrated YAHWEH SHÂMMAH – The Lord who is there. When the shepherds came to gaze upon the newborn infant they celebrated YAHWEH SHÂMMAH. When the wise men travelled far to pay homage to the young boy Jesus they celebrated YAHWEH SHÂMMAH.

When writing the account of the incarnation, the aged apostle John wrote, "The Word became flesh and dwelt among us, and we have seen His glory, glory as of the only Son from the Father, full of grace and truth" (John1:14 ESV). The truth is that there was a night, thousands of years ago, when God visited this planet in Jesus Christ.

When Yuri Gagarin, the first Russian astronaut, flew out of the earth's atmosphere, he was travelling with a special command from

Nikita Khrushchev, the first secretary of the Communist Party. Khrushchev had told him to have a look around to see if he could spot God anywhere. We well remember the words of the astronaut: "I can't see God anywhere!" Such is the limited view of man. The truth is we have YAHWEH SHÂMMAH because God is everywhere! We simply need to have our eyes opened to see. David would write,

"Our Lord, how majestic is your name in all the earth! You have set your glory above the heavens… When I look at your heavens, the work of your fingers, the moon and the stars, which you have set in place, what is man that you are mindful of him, and the son of man that you care for him? The heavens declare the glory of God, and the sky above proclaims his handiwork." (Psalm 8:1,3 and 19:1 ESV)

When the Christ child came into the earth, God lit up the sky with a unique star and the glory of an angelic choir. It was so visible. He was definitely there for all to see!

He is there in the Church

When we read the prophecies of Ezekiel concerning the new Temple of God, we pick up the idea that he is actually pointing towards the Church of Jesus Christ, His body, the new temple of God. God's presence can be discerned, seen and felt wherever His people are gathered. God loves to dwell with us.

Paul, writing to the Corinthian believers said, "Do you not know that you yourselves are God's temple and that God's Spirit lives in you?" (1 Corinthians 3:16 ESV). God's presence can be found wherever His Church is found! The Church is the body of Christ. We can be carriers of His presence and it is my conviction that in this dark world in which we live, the Church is meant to shine. Paul wrote to the church in Philippi that they should be, "blameless and innocent, children of God without blemish in the midst of a crooked and twisted generation, among whom you shine as lights in the world" (Philippians 2:15 ESV).

We are meant to be the light of the world. The Church is meant to be good news in word and deed and action, and as people see the Church, they ought to be able to proclaim "God is there". They ought to be able to say, like Jacob, "How awesome is this place! This is none other than the house of God, and this is the gate of heaven" (Genesis 28:17 ESV).

My belief is that each time we gather together and each time we go out, we should be carriers of the light of Jesus Christ. When we go into our homes and our places of work we can declare the kingdom of God is at hand and that God is here. We can begin to pray for people and we can believe to see them healed and we can declare God has come.

Our little pilgrimage

In September Irene and I decided that we would take a nice holiday. The church kindly helped us to go to New England and so we went with our friends Jack and Trish Groblewski. It was so beautiful there, especially as went in the autumn. While the girls went shopping, Jack and I decided to take some time out to go on a quest, visiting the historic sites of past revivals. There is a wonderful connection between the East coast of England and the East coast of America, especially New England. The Pilgrim Fathers originally hailed from Lincolnshire and when they eventually sailed from Plymouth, England, they came to a place on the East coast of America which they named New Plymouth. Jack and I visited there and saw "The Plymouth Rock" where the travellers prayed and thanked God for a safe voyage.

We took photographs of the gravestones of the great leaders of the revivals: Jonathan Edwards, the greatest theologian of his time, and David Brainerd, a passionate missionary to the Indians. We saw the grave of the famous George Whitfield who had preached to thousands, both here and in America. I personally wanted to visit Northampton in Massachusetts where Jonathan Edwards had been the minister. Edwards had experienced an awesome outpouring of the Holy Spirit during his time and the presence of God had been tangibly felt in the town. In fact, Edwards had written in his journal at the time that, "every household was filled with the presence of God." I wanted to see if there was any residue of that presence still there, after all these years!

As we walked the streets our hearts sank because the town was filled with all kinds of deviations and occult and New Age shops. We managed to find our way to the church where Jonathan Edwards had been the minister and there we found a clue as to why the presence and the glory of God had departed. There was a plaque there that spoke of a covenant that had been made by the people to evict Edwards because of his "extreme views about the presence and power of God". It all made sense and we were deeply saddened as we realized that the presence of God had literally been written out of that town.

In the beginning of the 20th century there was an incredible awakening in the valley of Wales. The presence of God was again tangible and at times it overpowered even the hardest of hearts. Today, if you visit there, you would not find any evidence of the visitation of God.

In Ezekiel 10:11 we read of the glory of God leaving the Temple. It is such a tragic picture. I think there must be nothing more terrible than a temple without the presence of God or a church without His presence. I am not sure I could live with a faith where the presence of God is not a daily living reality.

Later in the book, Ezekiel sees the glory of God return to the Temple. He also sees a little trickle of water coming from underneath the threshold of the temple, which gets deeper and deeper as it travels out. At first it gets to knee level, then as it gets higher it reaches to waist level and eventually becomes a river that has to be swum in because it is so deep. All this speaks of and signifies the healing and restorative presence of God.

I believe that God wants our cities to be filled with His presence. I believe that He wants our households to be filled with His presence. I believe He wants it to be like the days of Obed-edom, when the Ark of the Covenant was taken into his house. It is recorded in 2 Samuel 6:10-12 that because of the presence of the Ark, the LORD had blessed the house of Obed-edom.

"So David was not willing to take the ark of the LORD into the city of David. But David took it aside to the house of Obed-edom the Gittite. And the ark of the LORD remained in the house of Obed-edom the Gittite three months, and the LORD blessed Obed-edom and all his household." (2 Samuel 6:10-12 ESV)

Why such blessing? It was simply because the presence of the Lord was there. YAHWEH SHÂMMAH – The Lord who is there. In Ezekiel 43:1-5 we read,

"After this, the man brought me back around to the east gateway. Suddenly, the glory of the God of Israel appeared from the east. The sound of his coming was like the roar of rushing waters, and the whole landscape shone with his glory. This vision was just like the others I had seen, first by the Kebar River and then when he came to destroy Jerusalem. I fell face down on the ground. And the glory of the LORD came into the Temple through the east gateway. Then the Spirit took me up and brought me into the inner courtyard, and the glory of the LORD filled the Temple." (Ezekiel 43:1-5 NLT)

My prayer is that as followers of Jesus we will know what it is to be filled with His Holy Spirit. My prayer is that as the family of God we will never put up with being without the presence of God. We need to know that God is with us. God comes to save people, to set them free from sin, to give them a brand new life. He comes to forgive people who have made a mess of things, who perhaps in their minds have taken a u-turn away from Him.

There are many who attend church Sunday by Sunday who are, in reality, simply going through the motions. To such people God wants to become present in forgiveness and salvation, so that they experience for themselves the life and the presence of YAHWEH SHÂMMAH – The Lord who is there. He is the one who has made Himself present to us in the person of Jesus Christ. My prayer today is that people will come to know that God is alive and He can be intimately known in the person of Jesus Christ, the Son of God.

Reflect and pray…

No matter what I go through in life, in good or bad times, the Lord is there with me and His presence gives me rest.

"Thank you, Lord, for your name YAHWEH SHÂMMAH, which assures me that You are always there for me and with me. Thank you for countless testimonies through the ages of how you have drawn close to people in their different circumstances and changed things. You know exactly how to presence yourself with your people and you know that we ache for more of you throughout the earth. Come, Holy Spirit, and remind your Church again of your greatness and power! Amen."

3

The Lord is my Shepherd

One of the best-known and most loved passages to be found in the Bible is Psalm 23. For generations it has been used to bring comfort and strength both to those who know God personally and also those who don't. This evocative psalm, with its pastoral images of the Shepherd, green fields and still waters and its promise of loving protection and powerful anointing is an invitation to reach out to God in faith and trust that He is always leading us, always restoring us. When the burdens of life are overwhelming, Psalm 23 is a timely reminder that God is taking care of us as a shepherd cares for his sheep. In the Hebrew, the word for "Lord" in the first line – "The Lord is my Shepherd' – is "RA'AH" and means "to tend, to pasture, to graze and to feed". So we have YAHWEH RA'AH – The Lord is my Shepherd.

The whole psalm reads:

"The LORD is my shepherd; I shall not want.
He makes me lie down in green pastures.
He leads me beside still waters.
He restores my soul.
He leads me in paths of righteousness
for his name's sake.
Even though I walk through the valley of the shadow of death,
I will fear no evil,
for you are with me;

your rod and your staff,

they comfort me.

You prepare a table before me

in the presence of my enemies;

you anoint my head with oil;

my cup overflows.

Surely goodness and mercy shall follow me

all the days of my life,

and I shall dwell in the house of the LORD

forever." (Psalm 23 ESV)

Whilst some names of God speak to us about victory in battle or about His banner being over us in collective terms, this particular name is a very personal one. It is rooted in a relationship with the living God. David expresses his relationship with God here using intimate language such as "my Shepherd", acknowledging Him as the one who watches over his life, protecting him from harm, leading him into good places and providing for him. A shepherd has a special relationship with his sheep and David intimately knew the loving care of God as his shepherd.

In the 21st century we probably do not tend to think too much about sheep and shepherds. We almost certainly did not wake up this morning pondering pastoral scenes, unless of course last night we were counting sheep in order to get to sleep! The same was not true in biblical times.

Then, everything revolved around agriculture and farming methods, meaning that the Scriptures are full of references to these things. It is important, therefore, to have to have a bit of a background understanding of the significance of the phrase that is used for this name of God.

The word "sheep" appears in the Scriptures more than the word "grace." It is also found twice as many times as the word "pray." Does this surprise you? I am not drawing attention to it because I believe sheep are more important than grace and prayer, of course, but it does emphasize that the relationship between the shepherd and his sheep reflects the relationship between God and His people. References to sheep are in both the Old and New Testaments, with Jesus even referring to Himself as the Good Shepherd:

"I am the good shepherd. I know my own and my own know Me." (John 10:14 ESV)

Here the Greek word for "shepherd" is poimen and it can also be translated as "pastor", which in the Old Testament particularly referred to the feeding of sheep.   So when a pastor is caring for the people he is feeding them. When Jesus referred to Himself as a shepherd, it carried the same meaning: one who cares, one who feeds.

David wrote Psalm 23 based on his own experiences of being a shepherd in the Palestinian hills. He had first hand experience of how sheep behaved, what they needed and when, and how they needed protecting from predators.

David would have written with authority and understanding when he likened the Lord to a Shepherd overseeing His people Israel. In fact, throughout the Old Testament, many of the prophets identified the Lord as a Shepherd to the people of Israel, leading them strongly but gently out of captivity into the Promised Land.

In reality, the task of being a shepherd was not a very glamorous thing. Back in the day, shepherds were seen to be on one of the lowest rungs of society, possessing very little, having no voice and frequently being treated with disdain. That is why it is so very important to understand that when the Lord humbled Himself in being born to earth, coming into the dirt, He identified with the lowest of the low.

YAHWEH RA'AH – The Lord is my Shepherd. He came to where we are.

It is good to remember, too, that the very first group of people to hear about the news of the birth of Christ was a group of shepherds out on the Palestinian hills. Philip Yancey in his book, The Jesus I Never Knew writes of them,

"For just an instant the sky grew luminous with angels, yet who saw that spectacle? Illiterate hirelings who watched the flocks of others; 'nobodies' who failed to leave their names. Shepherds had such a randy reputation that proper Jews lumped them together with the 'godless,' restricting them to the outer courtyards of the temple."

Psalm 23 tells us something about ourselves

Let's look at Psalm 23 more closely and deepen our understanding of the name, YAHWEH RA'AH. As I mentioned earlier, Psalm 23 is read by both those who profess to be Christians and those who do not. The Word of God is accessible for all and whilst I don't always understand why someone who isn't in a relationship with God would find it meaningful, that is no reason to doubt that they can and do encounter the love of God through it.

By implication, if we say, "The Lord is my Shepherd" then we are admitting that we are sheep! If you have ever watched sheep for any length of time, you will know that they can be hilarious. One of them can decide to go off in a particular direction and all the others follow! This is not meant to be offensive, but this is a very good description of humanity. How easy it is to spend time chasing unimportant things and risk getting lost when what we really need is a shepherd to lead us. In fact, it is a very good thing to start off our day by saying that we need someone higher than ourselves to walk us through it. We need someone who can help us with this thing called life. We need the

Lord's support, guidance and, at times, we even need him to carry us
(see Isaiah 40:11 and 46:4).

Let me tell you a few more things I know about sheep.

First, did you know that sheep can only see for a distance of about
fourteen metres? That is not very far and may explain why they
sometimes give the impression they are staring into space! Sometimes,
like sheep, we would love to be able to see further than we do: to be
able to see into the future – but we cannot. As the sheep trusts the
shepherd to lead it into places it can't see, we must learn to do the same
with the Lord.

Secondly, as I have mentioned above, sheep are known for their
inane ability to wander without much purpose or direction. To know
the Lord as our Shepherd is to follow a leader who knows how to
lead. We can be foolish people at heart, wandering aimlessly through
our years, but God wants to bring us fresh revelation of His name,
YAHWEH RA'AH – The Lord is my Shepherd.

Many different studies in animal behaviour have concluded that
when left to their own devices, sheep behave in a disorganized and
random fashion. Under the watchful eye of a shepherd and with the
help of a good dog, they are capable of some pretty sharp manoeuvres!

Jesus picked up on this imagery in the New Testament when He
saw the crowds who were following Him. The Bible says that He
had compassion on them, because He saw them as sheep without a
shepherd. They were wandering, they did not know where they were
going and they seemed lost. As we think about these things, we can
learn a lot about ourselves. Without the guiding, protecting help of
our Shepherd, we are liable to wander without direction and run the
risk of damaging ourselves.

Thirdly, when a sheep topples over for some reason, it finds it virtually
impossible to get back up again without help. As it lies on the ground,
bewildered and bleating, this "cast sheep", as it is known, is completely

helpless and vulnerable to attack. Whenever we "fall" in life, we need help to get back up again. We should not hesitate to ask the Lord to help us and yet there is something dark and rebellious in each one of us that finds it difficult to ask. So often we try foolishly to lift ourselves up by relying on our own flesh, rather than admitting in humility that we need the help of God and others around us to try again.

The Bible teaches us that when Adam and Eve sinned, they fell from the grace and mercy of God. Theologians even call this event "the Fall." You could say then, that we have all become "cast sheep", lying helpless and needing a Saviour. Scripture refers to us as being like sheep who have "gone astray" (Isaiah 53:6), but the Lord has promised to look after us. One of my favourite passages on this is,

"The steps of a man are established by the LORD, when he delights in his way; though he fall, he shall not be cast headlong, for the LORD upholds his hand." (Psalm 37: 23-24 ESV)

The Great Shepherd comes looking for us and He "restores our soul." He picks us up, healing our wounds and bruises, helping us to stand again.

Psalm 23 tells us something about God

There are a number of key things that we can learn from this Psalm. First, God is personal. We touched on this earlier in this chapter, but I want to reiterate its importance. David does not say that the Lord is our shepherd. This Psalm was written from his personal experience of God coming through for him. David was able to say that the great Creator of all things, the great covenant-keeping God is my God, my shepherd. There must come a point when as Christians we realize that it is all about our individual relationship with the Lord and we begin to understand that we are not just a number on a roll, we are not just an accident that happened, but rather God has specifically made us in His own image for relationship, because He loves us so desperately.

Secondly, God has authority. Images of the Egyptian Pharaohs often show them carrying a shepherd's crook in one hand which represented not only the care of the ruler but also his authority. When the shepherd's crook was seen, it showed that the shepherd of the nation was in charge over His people. As we consider this Scripture, we realize that the Lord as a Shepherd has ultimate and loving authority over our lives when we surrender to Him and let Him lead us.

Thirdly, God is loving. The tender loving care of the Lord towards His people is evident throughout Scripture and this Psalm is a beautiful example of it. The biblical picture of a shepherd is that of one who both leads and follows his flock. In Psalm 78:70-72 we read how David, the shepherd of Israel, was called by God from the care of the sheep.

"He chose David his servant and took him from the sheepfolds; from following the nursing ewes he brought him to shepherd Jacob, his people, Israel his inheritance. With an upright heart he shepherded them and guided them with a skilful hand." (Psalm 78:70-72 ESV)

In different translations of the Bible the word "following" is substituted by other words, such as "the care of" (NASB) and "tending" (NIV). The word is achar and it means "the hind, the following part", taken from a root word meaning "to remain behind, to tarry". The sense here then is that David was literally "following the sheep" (see also Genesis 33:14 and 2 Samuel 7:8). From this we learn that the biblical shepherd is not so up front that the sheep lose sight of him, but neither is he driving them so hard that it becomes oppressive. His prime concern is for their welfare, not so much the route to be taken or the speed required to get there. He obviously loves the sheep and will carry the weaker ones. He is patient, walking at their pace and he is gentle with the expectant mothers and youngsters (see also Philippians 3:17, 4:9; 1 Timothy 4:12; 2 Timothy 3:10; 1 Thessalonians 1:5-7, 2:7:12). Notice the "fathering and mothering" in the last reference. This is an accurate picture of the shepherding heart of God being reflected in the heart of David.

Isaiah 40:11 says that God,

"...will feed his flock like a shepherd. He will carry the lambs in his arms, holding them close to his heart. He will gently lead the mother sheep with their young." (Isaiah 40:11 NLT)

Here then, we have the picture of a caring shepherd God who is on our side, who fights our enemies, who is overseeing our lives, who has authority over us but who is also deeply caring and deeply loving. The embodiment of the Father's love for us is found in Jesus who demonstrated it fully when He lived among us.

It is in verse 4 where the style of the Psalm changes. Between verses 1-3, David writes about the Lord. In verse 4 he starts to write about the valley of the shadow of death or deep darkness, and he finds himself talking to the Lord. Why the change? I believe it is simply that when David remembered his own valley experiences, he remembered, or called to mind, the closeness of God to him during them, and his instinct is to turn to God in prayer instead of commenting about Him.

I wonder how you think about God in your daily life? Do you think of Him as being remote and distant, somewhere far off, or do you see Him as close to you, even when you are having a really tough time? God is with us all the time in the presence of His Holy Spirit.

As we walk through deathly shadows, we are not alone. God has promised that He will never leave us, just as a shepherd would never leave his sheep. God is 100% committed to staying with us through thick and thin, dark and light, and no experience we go through will ever keep Him away.

Finally, we learn that God is healing. David prays to God as the one who "anoints". For us, living in New Testament times, this is more likely to be a picture of the anointing power of the Holy Spirit. In the Middle East, however, it is a very beautiful image of the intimate care of the shepherd. Very often a sheep would attract ticks and parasites that would climb into their nostrils and ears causing great distress. They would rub their heads against trees and walls in an attempt to get some relief. When the shepherd saw this happening, he would take a mixture of oils and liberally anoint their heads with it. As the oil seeped into their nostrils and ears, the parasites were flushed out, the wounds were soothed and they were restored to calm. What a wonderful picture of the tenderness of a shepherd!

In today's world there are plenty of parasites out there that would worry and distress us. There are things that niggle us and cause us to fret. There are things that harm us, addictions that lock us into destructive patterns and burdens we carry that become too heavy to bear alone. The Lord is our shepherd and He wants to pour oil upon our heads, dealing with the things that work against us.

Interestingly, within this Psalm lie references to other names of God. Not only is there YAHWEH RA'AH – the Lord is my Shepherd, but there is YAHWEH JIREH: "the Lord will provide" as David writes in verse 1, "I shall not want." Then in verse 2 we read, "He makes me lie down in green pastures, He leads me beside quiet waters." It is a picture of wonderful peace, which is reflected in the name, YAHWEH SHALOM – the God who is our peace. Following on from that we have, in the first part of verse 3, "He restores my soul" – a picture of healing, refreshment and restoration contained in the name YAHWEH RAPHAH – the Lord who is our Healer. Then, in the second part of verse 3 we read, "He guides me in paths of righteousness (or "right paths") for His name's sake" and so He is revealed as YAHWEH TSIDKENU – the Lord our Righteousness. Continuing to verse 5 David writes, "You prepare a table before me in the presence of my enemies," which reveals the name YAHWEH NISSI: "the Lord is our Banner". Finally, in verse 6 we read, "...and I will dwell in the house of the Lord forever" which alludes to YAHWEH SHÂMMAH – the Lord who is there.

It is wonderful to see how the names of God are interwoven in this beautiful piece of poetry. It seems that David is saying, "This is my God. He is the God who brings life to me, He is my shepherd, He provides for everything that I need, He leads me in a way of peace, He is my righteousness, He is my healer, He restores my soul, He replenishes me, He restores me, He protects me, He is a banner over me, and what's more, He is there right until the very end."

Psalm 23 tells us something about our journey

The word "journey" has always intrigued me. Life is, at times, simultaneously a complex, wonderful, confusing, mediocre, stressful and blissful journey – and this is the same for every human being whether we know Christ or not. I do not think that there is anyone reading this who would ever claim that they have made it, that they have arrived such that their entire life is sorted, but the truth is that if we are followers of Christ then life can be a very exciting journey. As we travel with God we should be maturing in our faith, step by step. We are meant to grow, becoming more and more like Jesus every day. People around us should be able to notice how we resemble the amazing character of Jesus that we see revealed in the gospels. This is the one purpose of the Holy Spirit in our lives – to conform us into the image of Christ.

As we get older, there is an unspoken expectation that we will slow down and become more nostalgic than prophetic. We must not accept this! We must shake off the caricature of being boring and grumpy in our old age. Why? Because the Bible paints a totally different picture. Caleb, for example, was the ripe old age of eighty-five when he started looking for new land to possess. We read in the psalms that the righteous flourish and grow, and that they will be,

"...like a tree planted by the rivers of water, that brings forth its fruit in its season." (Psalm 1:3 NKJV)

As we grow older on our journey, we will find that we will probably have more time on our hands – time that we can spend with God, during which we can receive more shaping discipline from His hand and much more of His love and grace into our lives. We should be aiming to grow and develop in our knowledge and understanding of the Word of God. Our goal should be that when we get old and frail, we are not put on the shelf, but we become an inspiration and a testimony to the younger generation.

I have to speak this to myself now, as I begin to grow older. I have to make a daily choice to refuse to become a grumpy, boring and irrelevant old man and I believe that God wants each one of us to be a light into our world. I believe that He wants us to understand that on each season of our journey, He is with us. He is YAHWEH RA'AH – The Lord is my Shepherd.

In some ways Psalm 23 is the diary of a sheep! The journey begins in the early morning with a picture of peace and tranquillity, waking up to the knowledge that the Shepherd is there and all is well. As the hours pass, we are in the heat of the noonday sun, where there is need for refreshment and green pastures and still waters that cool. As the day progresses into the shadows of the evening and the darkness of night, the deep valleys and a sense of foreboding are comforted by the promise of the nearness of God. Of course, the Psalm is not primarily a day in the life of a sheep: it is much more profound than that! David takes us on a journey throughout all the seasons of our lives. We find, however, that God is not only at the beginning of that journey, He is also with us right now and He will be with us until its end. Verse by verse, this Psalm assures us that we are safe and secure in the care of our Shepherd and there is nothing to fear.

Fear is one of the key emotions that most negatively affects our journey with Jesus. Psalm 23 confronts fear head on by asserting the tender care of our Shepherd who will never leave us and gently leads us through the seasons of our life. Many of the commentaries that I have read that cover this Psalm refer to this issue of fear and anxiety. The spirit of fear can keep us in bondage for years and often we can even forget what we were originally afraid of. Winston Churchill once wrote about a conversation he'd had with an elderly gentleman who confessed to him that he had been plagued by many worries and fears in his long life, most of which had never happened!

Fear is so damaging that it robs us of our future. In this Psalm David writes, "I will fear no evil," based on his own experiences fighting wild animals as a young shepherd boy. Not only that, but of course as a young man he faced the intimidation and power of Goliath, a nine foot tall giant, bringing him down with no armour and a slingshot. In the same way, if we have faced a few of our own giants then like David, we do not really have to worry about the future. Has God ever let you down in your past? No. Will He be with you in your future? Yes. Whatever mountains you face, whatever valleys you are going through, whatever giants you have to face, God is alongside you.

God has not only given us His Holy Spirit to shepherd us through life, He has also given us each other for blessing and encouragement. We function so much better when we are connected to others who are also journeying through life with Him.

This Psalm shows us something of the nature of the Church as well as the individual. It is possible to have fellowship together around a table surrounded by the presence of our enemies and it is possible to know the anointing of the oil of God, the Holy Spirit, over our corporate lives, within the fellowship of God's people. We were not destined to journey alone: God has given us each other.

There is provision for the journey

It is important to remember that God gives us His resources to keep walking with Him through life. He provides for us, protects us and prepares us. David knew that in God he would lack for nothing – God would provide for all his needs – and much later in his life he testified to it:

"I have been young and now I am old, yet I have not seen the righteous forsaken or his children begging for bread." (Psalm 37:25 ESV)

So too, we have this same assurance that God will take care of us. God not only provides for us in material ways, He provides for us spiritually and emotionally as well. David testifies that, "He makes me lie down in green pastures." This is an apposite word for life in the 21st century which is full of stress and driven-ness. To know that God invites us to lie down and take rest is an enormous blessing.

The text then says, "He leads me beside quiet waters." This is so evocative, we can almost hear the rippling of the stream as we read it. In the green pastures by the quiet waters is where we relax into who God is, soaking in His presence. The Bible tells us that there is a place of quiet rest near to the heart of God; there is a place where we can know profound peace in our souls. I believe that our Shepherd has provision for the journey at every stage of our lives and even when we come to the valley times, we will discover He provides everything that we need – body, soul and spirit.

In Matthew's gospel, Jesus says to His anxious disciples, "Do not be anxious about your life, what you will eat or what you will drink, nor about your body, what you will put on. Is not life more than food, and the body more than clothing?' (Matthew 6:25 ESV)

He said that our heavenly Father sees to it that we are provided for. Anxiety can creep up on any of us at any time for all sorts of reasons, and in times of crisis we can be plagued with doubts, questioning whether God notices and loves us enough to provide for us. Jesus asks us to simply trust Him on the journey. The Bible is full of examples of the provision of God for His people on their journeys, from manna in the morning to rain in times of drought. We must learn to trust what has been written so that as we walk through our difficult times, as we peer into our future, we can put our hand into the hand of YAHWEH RA'AH – the Lord who is our Shepherd, and feel safe.

There is protection for the journey

In Psalm 23:4 David writes that, "Even though I walk through the valley of the shadow of death, I will fear no evil." I wonder how many of us can say that with a strong measure of reality? It is not something we can just decide to do in our minds. Overcoming fear is not done with logic. These words are a God-breathed revelation that we need to let sink into our hearts. When the bad news hits us, when we find ourselves face to face with death and its shadows, He does not and will not leave us. He has promised to be with us in the ups and downs of our lives, never abandoning us, always fighting for us.

When the enemy comes to attack us and harass us, as a Good

Shepherd He is there to protect us on every front with His "rod" and His "staff". The shepherd's rod was designed to combat the enemy. It was like a cudgel that the shepherd would wield to beat off wild animals that attempted to attack the sheep. When we are helpless, God comes to fight our battles with His rod, dealing personally with our enemies on our behalf.

Then there is the staff. This piece of wood was not so much for the enemies of the flock, but for the sheep themselves. The rod was for defending the sheep and the staff was for disciplining the sheep. The staff was employed to hook the sheep and pull them back to safety whenever they found themselves in danger.

Most of us do not like this "pulling back" process. We do not like getting "hooked" by the shepherd. But we need to understand it is only because of the Shepherd's love for us that He hooks us and keeps us in order. It is His amazing love that both disciplines and protects us day by day. It is for this reason that the job of a shepherd was not one that was often sought after – it often involved personal danger and sacrifice. As the Good Shepherd, Jesus Himself said that He had come to lay down His life for the sheep (John 10:15). The promise is that as we journey with the Shepherd of our souls, we are never going to get totally swamped; we are never going to get badly hurt because He promises to protect us. Keeping our enemies at bay with His rod He will fight our battles, and with His staff He will hook us back, looking after us, disciplining us and protecting us. What a God we have!

There is preparation for the journey

God prepares us for the journey at every level. There is preparation in the morning, there is preparation at midday and there is preparation when the shadows fall. In verse 5 we read,

"You prepare a table before me in the presence of my enemies, You anoint my head with oil, my cup overflows. Surely goodness and love will follow me all the days of my life and I will dwell in the house of the Lord forever." (Psalm 23:6 ESV)

The Bible tells us that He has also prepared good works for us to walk into:

"For we are his workmanship, created in Christ Jesus for good works, which God prepared beforehand, that we should walk in them." (Ephesians 2:10 ESV)

In this Psalm is a wonderful picture of a table that has been laid for us. God loves to provide tables for us since He loves to see His people feasting at the places He has prepared. The prophet Isaiah paints a fabulous image:

"On this mountain the Lord of hosts will make for all peoples a feast of rich food, a feast of well-aged wine, of rich food full of marrow, of aged wine well refined." (Isaiah 25:6-ESV)

It is God's love that will bring us there. He will provide a table for us with fellowship and feasting, pouring over us the oil of anointing.

I find it incredible that David saw this oil of anointing hundreds of years before that particular day of Pentecost when the Spirit came upon the disciples who were waiting in the upper room. In the Old Testament, when the oil of anointing was poured on someone, it was poured liberally on the head and it would run all the way down their robes to the floor. Aaron certainly experienced it that way:

"Behold, how good and pleasant it is when brothers dwell in unity!

It is like the precious oil on the head, running down on the beard, on the beard of Aaron, running down on the collar of his robes!" (Psalm 133:1-2 ESV)

Jesus told the disciples to wait in Jerusalem until they received the promise of the Father. There was preparation for the future, there was power for everything they were going to face in the future, and He anointed their heads with oil and their cups overflowed with blessing. The same promise applies to us. The Shepherd has prepared everything that we need as He is YAHWEH RA'AH – the Lord is my Shepherd. We have a future that is secure and we have the promise that we will dwell in the house of the Lord forever!

Reflect and pray...
On my life's journey, whatever it holds, I can always rely on the companionship and love of my Shepherd.

Lord, I want to let you lead me and I want to know you are following me. Thank you that your presence is always with me, that you know what is best for me and when I need you to, you will defend and protect me. I want to give you my anxieties and fears and let you lead me to a place of stillness and calm. Please anoint me now with the oil of joy and let it fill my heart. Amen.

4

The Lord is my Provider

We know that we will never be able to fully understand God. In fact, God Himself says to us,

"For my thoughts are not your thoughts, neither are your ways my ways..." (Isaiah 58:8 ESV)

Through this He is reminding us that however hard we try, we will not be able to make sense of how He thinks and acts. Michael Casey, a Cistercian abbot, wrote, "In the presence of the Holy, we quickly become aware that our rational mind is a much blunted instrument...". However, Scripture points the way for us as we journey with Him.

In this chapter I want to focus solely on a particular passage from the Bible that I believe will expand and deepen our understanding of another of God's names: YAHWEH JIREH – the Lord will see. Very often, the Hebrew is translated as "the Lord will provide" which is also correct, but for the purposes of this book, I have chosen "the Lord will see". The passage we will be using to illustrate this wonderful name of God – Genesis 22:1-19 – contains many profound elements.

Before we begin to look at it in depth, perhaps you could read it slowly and prayerfully in order to help place this name of God in context. It is not an easy story to read in some ways, as it deals with issues that are unfamiliar to our Western culture. In our struggle to understand the more challenging passages in Scripture, we can be tempted to dismiss what does not make sense. My prayer is that the inspiration of the Holy Spirit will lead and guide you as we walk through this holy ground.

The journey

I want briefly to take you back a few chapters in Genesis in order to lay a foundation for what is to come in this passage. The interaction between God and Abraham concerning Isaac in Genesis chapter 22 falls within the context of a journey that Abraham himself was taking with God which began in chapter 12 when God called him, saying,

"Go from your country and your kindred and your father's house to the land that I will show you. And I will make of you a great nation, and I will bless you and make your name great, so that you will be a blessing. I will bless those who bless you, and him who dishonours you I will curse, and in you all the families of the earth shall be blessed." (Genesis 12:1-3 ESV)

God's instruction to Abraham to sacrifice Isaac did not come suddenly like a bolt out of the blue, it came in the context of some extremely important lessons that Abraham had already learned after he had obeyed His call. In other words, Abraham was already a friend of God; he had become acquainted with God's ways and had learned to trust Him in all things. Because of this relationship, God was able to entrust Abraham with this earth-shattering test.

When God first called him, Abraham was actually called Abram, which means, "exalted father". So from the beginning, when he first encountered God, Abram was destined for something important. Somewhere on his journey, at a pivotal moment, God changed his name to Abraham and his destiny was then sealed.

His life, and the lives of those around him, was transformed and the promises of God burst into life. There are some key points I want to draw out from Abraham's life:

God calls ordinary people

When the call came to Abram from God, it is clear from Scripture that it was a radical call! Abram originally came from a foreign land with foreign gods, called Ur which was in Mesopotamia. He had an existing family and to move away from Ur meant separating from his father's household.

"Now the LORD said to Abram, 'Go from your country and your kindred and your father's house to the land that I will show you.'" (Genesis 12:1 ESV)

We know that at this time in history, the city of Ur was dedicated to the worship of the moon-god Nannar. Faussett's Bible Dictionary states that, "Ur was also a cemetery and city of tombs, doubtless because of its sacred character, from whence the dead were brought to it from vast distances for 1,800 years." In short, it was not a very cheerful place! The name "Ur" literally means "fire or flame" and interestingly, there is an apocryphal story about the call of Abram in both the Koran and the Talmud which states, "…Abraham miraculously escaped out of the flames into which Nimrod or other idolatrous persecutors threw him."

God in His sovereignty called Abram out of obscurity, offering him very little information on what was ahead. Abram was required to listen and obey in faith rather than have all the stages of the process laid out before him. God was calling him to an adventure, but without giving him time for the preparation that would normally happen when a move to another country was planned. Stephen records in Acts 7:3 that God said to Abram,

"Go from your country and your kindred and your father's house to the land that I will show you." (Genesis 12:1 ESV)

The writer to the Hebrews also adds that,

"...he went out, not knowing where he was going." (Hebrews 11:8 ESV)

Most commentators agree that Abram's response to this call of God was prompt. God did not, however, reveal the end result to him, but called him into a daily dependent walk. The leave and the go aspects were important and clear, but the where was not.

Nothing but faith can compel a man to leave his familiar world and to start a pilgrimage to an unseen better place. The NIV Bible Commentary says, "to leave the certainties one knows and go out into what is quite uncertain – relying on nothing but the Word of God – is the essence of faith." It was only when Abram reached his destination that God told him, "This is it" and then promised him the land.

This is clearly an occasion where Abram walked by faith and not by sight (2 Corinthians 5:7) or as one Puritan divine wrote, "Abraham went out, not knowing where he went, but he did know with whom he went."

It was exactly the same in the New Testament when Jesus called His disciples. He said to them,

"Follow me, and I will make you fishers of men." (Matthew 4:19 ESV)

Such was the strength of the call that they literally left everything and followed Him as He journeyed.

God calls ordinary people and He begins a walk with them. Perhaps you could for a moment reflect on the day you were first called – the day that you first responded to God; the day when you were challenged to forsake everything and follow Him. Whether it was an easy or difficult decision for you, offer your thanks now for that life-changing moment when you said to Him, "Yes, I'll follow you."

As Abram continues on his journey, he learns more and more about God, as do we. He finds that he can trust Him more as time passes and as he begins to reflect on times of God's faithfulness to him. He did not know about the tests and challenges ahead, but as he focussed on his step-by-step, day by day, walk with God, he grew in stature and faith.

After his call in Genesis chapter 12, Scripture reveals more of what Abram was really like. As a character, he had some rough edges that required smoothing. His morality was questionable and his relationship with his wife was far from great.

In short, God needed to re-shape him if he was to enter into his destiny as the father of many. This should be an encouragement to us. God tends to take rough lumps of clay out of the darkness of the earth and then He begins to shape and fashion it into something beautiful.

Abram is learning something about God as he walks with Him. He learns that God takes hold of ordinary people and moulds them into something new that reflects His nature and character. He also learns that there is grace in this process as God leaves room for the pains that accompany change and new birth.

One year, we called our annual Grapevine celebration "The Journey" because we sensed that God was taking us somewhere new that we had not visited before. No matter how long we walk with God, there is always that sense that we do not know exactly where we are going, but we know it is an exciting journey. It is a journey of faith and it is taking us to bigger and better things.

God has good plans for us

In Genesis chapter 15:1 we read,

"After these things the word of the Lord came to Abram in a vision:
' Fear not, Abram, I am your shield; your reward shall be very great.'"
(Genesis 15:1 ESV)

This is a crucial chapter in the beginning of his journey. Here, God
both promises to be his protection and also assures him that his reward
will be very great. In the same way, when we are called, we have a
promise of protection and a promise of prosperity. This blessing of
prosperity was not to be restricted to just Abram, however, it would
reach far and wide across the nations. In His generosity and love, God
was going to bless Abram in order to touch the nations of the earth.

   At this point in time, Abram had no son. Because he had no heir
all Abram's worldly goods would be left to his servant, Eliezer. It was
a sensible and well thought through choice on Abram's part, given the
circumstances. But God had other ideas. He tells Abram that Eliezer
will not be his heir, but he will have a son who will come from his
own body. In addition, God gives him two more wonderful promises,
this time to do with posterity. He will not only have a son, but his
descendants will be too numerous to count! God says to him,

"'Look toward heaven, and number the stars, if you are able to number
them.' Then he said to him, 'So shall your offspring be.'" (Genesis 15:5
ESV)

Well, this was a challenge! Both Abram and his wife, Sarai, were
elderly, and she was well past the age of child bearing. It all looked
impossible, but Abram made the choice to take God at His word.

It is interesting to note at this point that several barren women in the Bible gave birth to significant children through supernatural answers to prayer. Sarah gave birth to Isaac (Genesis 21:1-2); Rachel gave birth to Jacob and Esau (Genesis 25:21-26); Rachel gave birth to Joseph (Genesis: 29:31 and 30:22-24); Manoah's wife gave birth to Samson (Judges 13:2-5); Hannah gave birth to Samuel (1 Samuel 1:2, 5, 17-20) and Elizabeth gave birth to John the Baptist (Luke 1:7, 13-17, 24, 36, 57).

In his letter to the Romans, the apostle Paul comments on Abraham's faith over this issue:

"That is why it depends on faith, in order that the promise may rest on grace and be guaranteed to all his offspring—not only to the adherent of the law but also to the one who shares the faith of Abraham, who is the father of us all, as it is written, 'I have made you the father of many nations'—in the presence of the God in whom he believed, who gives life to the dead and calls into existence the things that do not exist. In hope he believed against hope, that he should become the father of many nations, as he had been told, 'So shall your offspring be.' He did not weaken in faith when he considered his own body, which was as good as dead (since he was about a hundred years old), or when he considered the barrenness of Sarah's womb. No distrust made him waver concerning the promise of God, but he grew strong in his faith as he gave glory to God, fully convinced that God was able to do what He had promised." (Romans 4:16-21 ESV)

There are a number of key points here. First, the Scripture says that "in hope he believed against hope." A more literal translation is, "who beyond hope on hope believed…". Kenneth Wuest wrote, "his situation was beyond human hope, but in spite of that he rested it upon hope in God." In a hopeless situation, Abraham hoped in his heavenly Friend.

Secondly, we read that, "he did not weaken in faith as he considered his own body which was as good as dead (since he was about a hundred years old) or when he considered the barrenness of Sarah's womb." The word "consider" literally means "to consider carefully and closely in order to understand more fully".

Abram did not seek to escape from the facts – he closely examined them and he did not allow the truth of what was in front of him to rob him of faith in what could be. The verse goes on to say that, "no distrust made him waver…". Again, this is more literally translated "he did not decide by unbelief". Kenneth Wuest puts it this way: "he did not vacillate between belief and unbelief."

Thirdly, the Scripture says that "he grew strong in his faith." The phrase "grew strong" in the Greek language is passive and is better translated, "he was strengthened in his faith". In other words, God was pleased with the stand of faith that Abraham was taking and decided to add more strength to it.

Kenneth Wuest also writes, quoting Vincent, "Faith apprehends as a real fact what is not revealed to the senses. It rests on that fact, acts upon it, and is upheld by it in the face of all that seems to contradict it. Faith is real seeing."

With every step that he takes, Abram learns something about God. He learns that God calls people, he learns that God is good and that God wants to bless people. He learns that God's plans and purposes for his life are great and, if he will trust implicitly in Him, then God has a whole destiny for him which will bring blessing to nations.

I believe that everyone has a destiny in God. We are not designed simply to go through seventy or eighty years living a mediocre life. We are meant to be men and women of influence, blessed by God and a blessing to those around us in our churches and in our neighbourhoods.

We cannot make it happen ourselves

Abram and Sarai actually got sidetracked on this one for a little while, thinking that they could help God out by pre-empting some things. Sarai offered her servant Hagar to Abram and, as a result, Ishmael was born (Genesis16:1-4). This was the custom of the day, but the immediate result was strife in the home and the long-term result was the progeny who inherited Hagar's defiant spirit. I believe the conflict over the land of Israel can be traced back to the various legacies left by illegitimacy. Notice the behaviour of Lot's two daughters after they had left Sodom in Genesis 19:30-38, for example. Their dabbling in the purposes of God resulted in two children called Moab and Ben-ammi, the father of the Ammonites. Both boys went on to become a source of long-term pain for the people of God.

Abram had to learn to trust God through his mistakes. His journey of faith required him to learn what to do and what not to do. Abram will soon face a test to see how much he has learned. The biggest test of his life, to come in Genesis 22, will prove the depth of Abram's relationship with God.

God will only test what has already been constructed within us. Exams come at the end of a period of learning. Many of us know that it is highly likely that what we say about our faith will eventually be tested. We often say things in the flush of blessing, but when times get tough, it is then that the levels of our faith are truly seen. It is on the mountains that we see the revelation of God, but it is in the valleys that we discover the depth of our relationship with God.

God can change and transform us

In Genesis 17:1-5 we find God coming to Abram again, reaffirming the covenant that He originally made with him. It is at this point that

Abram becomes Abraham.

"When Abram was ninety-nine years old the LORD appeared to
Abram and said to him, 'I am God Almighty; walk before me, and
be blameless, that I may make my covenant between me and you, and
may multiply you greatly.' Then Abram fell on his face. And God said
to him, 'Behold, my covenant is with you, and you shall be the father
of a multitude of nations. No longer shall your name be called Abram,
but your name shall be Abraham, for I have made you the father of a
multitude of nations.'" (Genesis 17:1-5 ESV)

The name "Abram" means "exalted father," but the name "Abraham"
means "father of a multitude". By changing his name thus, God is
saying to him that he is already a father figure, but that the dimension
and capacity of those he fathers will be increased.

When God takes hold of a person, He takes the raw material of
their life and then starts to shape and form them into something
bigger. In New Testament terms, God's intent is to take the essence
of our lives, already made in His image, and transform us fully into
the likeness of Christ. At the same time, our capacity and sphere of
influence increases. Abram becomes Abraham.

God then speaks to Sarai, Abraham's wife. Later in chapter 17, we
read these words"

"And God said to Abraham, 'As for Sarai your wife, you shall not call her
name Sarai, but Sarah shall be her name. I will bless her, and moreover,
I will give you a son by her. I will bless her, and she shall become
nations; kings of peoples shall come from her.'" (Genesis17:15-16
ESV)

The name "Sarai" means "a princess", but "Sarah" means "the princess"

– denoting a change of status from one of many, to the predominant or the primary one.

I wonder what Sarah felt when she received her new name. To be called "princess" must have been special, but to be called "the princess" must have been amazing! Bear in mind here that she was very advanced in years, so maybe that day she looked through the wrinkles to see "the princess" that God saw she was.

Just like Sarah, we need to remember to see ourselves as God sees us. Often we view who we are as individuals through the filter of our past experiences, when the truth is that we are defined by how God sees us: unique and precious. Not only that, He sees what He is making us into – more and more conformed to the image of His Son, Jesus, day by day, year by year.

"And we know that for those who love God all things work together for good, for those who are called according to His purpose. For those whom He foreknew He also predestined to be conformed to the image of his Son." (Romans 8:28-29 ESV)

God is committed to changing our lives for the better and one day we shall be like Him.

God is just

In the story of his life so far, we have read how Abraham has learned that God is both good and kind. As we come to Genesis chapter 19, Abraham will learn that God is just.

In the account, Abraham "barters" with God over the fate of the city of Sodom. God reveals to Abraham that He is going to destroy Sodom because the perverted behaviour that is practised there is abhorrent to Him. When Abraham begins to intercede for the city, asking for

God's mercy if a certain amount of righteous people are found within it, God seems to respond positively to Abraham's "bartering" and the numbers come down. It seems that he is tapping into God's reluctance to bring judgement. God is willing to change His mind if Abraham can find a few righteous people in this dark city. Of course, no one was found and God's judgement fell, meaning that Sodom was annihilated and the darkness extinguished. Abraham learned the hard way that judgement is God's strange work of mercy.

God keeps His promises

We now come back for a moment to Genesis 18 where Abraham learns that God keeps His promises. This chapter is one of those fun passages for me! There are three mystical visitors who arrive one day and Abraham offers them hospitality. A conversation ensues on the subject of Sarah. Immediately after their initial enquiry about her whereabouts, the visitors suddenly speak out a prophetic word that she will be holding her own baby within a year. Sarah is listening in to the conversation from inside the tent and she begins to chuckle. It was not a faith-filled chuckle however; it was more a "you must be joking" kind of laugh. The Lord heard it and said to Abraham, "Why did Sarah laugh and doubt?". Then He spoke these words:

"Is anything too hard for the LORD? At the appointed time I will return to you, about this time next year, and Sarah shall have a son." (Genesis 18:14 ESV)

We read later that,

"The Lord visited Sarah as He had said, and the Lord did to Sarah as He had promised. And Sarah conceived and bore Abraham a son in his old age at the time of which God had spoken to him." (Genesis 21:1 ESV)

Abraham called the infant "Isaac", which means, "He laughs". This time, it was the laughter of heaven that came into the household. The promise had been fulfilled, the son had been delivered and everyone would now live happily ever after. Up to this point it is the perfect story of how God takes somebody out of obscurity, into a new land, blessing him all the way. As each chapter has unfolded we have seen the blessing, glory and promise that rested upon this family. The promise given by God to Abram in Genesis chapter 12 had been fulfilled and Abraham held the child that was promised, breathing and gurgling in his arms. Perhaps he reflected on his journey and smiled with contentment at its happy ending. Except, we know it does not end here! All that Abraham had learned about God up to this point was the prelude to the test of his life that lay just around the corner.

The test

In Genesis chapter 22 God speaks to Abraham and asks him to take his son Isaac to a place called Mount Moriah. There he is to offer him as a burnt offering. By now Abraham has learned to discern the voice of God, so he is in no doubt as to who is speaking to him. However, this only serves to intensify the pain that is to enter his soul. This is no demonic voice; neither is it a fabrication of his own thoughts; it is the sound of heaven. In God's command, there is a poignant description of Isaac that is crystal clear:

"Take your son, your only son Isaac, whom you love…" (Genesis 22:2 ESV)

God is striking at the heart of the matter. Abraham is so in love, so enamoured with his son that he has lost sight of the God who gave the boy to him in the first place.

As 21st century parents we cannot easily grasp this command from God. It will help to provide some contextual background at this point. In Abraham's day, human sacrifice was a common occurrence and was rife in Caananite religions. It was not the mode of sacrifice that was strange to Abraham, but the identity of the one who was to be sacrificed – his only son – the son of promise.

However, Abraham had also learned that whatever happened to him, God would always be there for him. He learned that God could be trusted; that He is good; that He would never want to take life away. In fact, God is the one who wants to give life – in abundance! So, this part of Abraham's journey was a step of gut-wrenching obedience and raw trust.

The Bible teaches that obedience is better than sacrifice. Today, if we were faced with the scenario that faced Abraham, many of us would have far more questions than he did, but we read that he just got up early in the morning and went to that place, suggesting that his inner heart-wrestling took place during the night. By the morning, his decision was made.

There have been perhaps many times when God has spoken to us when we have had to wrestle with what He has said. We have been unsure whether it was or wasn't God who was speaking to us. But, looking at the example of Abraham, we see a man who embraced the word of God, even though there was pain and darkness ahead of him, knowing that God would meet him in that darkness.

God will be there when we need Him. This truth we will discover more and more as we journey with Him. We will discover that He is indeed YAHWEH JIREH. One of the greatest adventures of life is to get to know Him. Paul the apostle wrote that his desire was that,

"I may know him and the power of His resurrection." (Philippians 3:10 ESV)

Can we really trust Him? If we can answer yes to that question then we will go anywhere, we will do anything and we will face anything. If He can really be trusted, when we get to that place of trial, we will know that He will be there for us.

Let us think again about what Abraham is being asked to sacrifice. He is being asked to put to death the promise for which he has waited for years. He is being told to sacrifice Isaac, his son, the one who has filled his heart with laughter. He has been told that he must give the very best thing that he has. He must give his only son! I have to ask myself how I would have responded to such a request from God.

I remember as a young boy how I attended a Billy Graham crusade. I remember when they sang the famous hymn "I surrender all". I would outwardly sing it with them, but inwardly I would be surrendering as much as I could cope with, which seemed at the time like only a small amount. Think carefully about these words, "I surrender all" for a moment. "All" can mean family, job, finances, future, ministry, life, everything! Perhaps Abraham once said to God, "Everything I have is yours" and God took him at his word, testing it in the most serious way possible? Nevertheless, Abraham sets off up the mountain with Isaac, two servants and some wood.

Verse 5 is the key verse to understanding this passage.

"Then Abraham said to his young men, 'Stay here with the donkey; I and the boy will go over there and worship and come again to you.'" (Genesis 22:5 ESV)

Here is Abraham's faith. He is telling the servants that both of them are going to return after this act of sacrifice. He is saying that he is going to slay his son and that they are both going to return. This is implicit faith. This is amazing faith.

Now maybe Abraham had an inkling that God was not intending to follow things through to the end, but nevertheless he remained totally obedient, even to the picking up of the knife. He was obedient because if God was going to keep His promise, as God always did in his experience, then even if the child died, God would have to resurrect him.

In the letter to the Hebrews, Abraham appears a number of times as an example of a man of faith. In particular, it is written,
"By faith Abraham, when he was tested, offered up Isaac, and he who had received the   promises was in the act of offering up his only son, of whom it was said, 'through Isaac shall your offspring be named.' He considered that God was able even to raise him from the dead, from which, figuratively speaking, he did receive him back." (Hebrews11:17-19 ESV)

The Bible teaches us that he would have sacrificed his son, believing the promise that God had given to him was sure. That is authentic faith.

"And Isaac said to his father Abraham, 'My father!' And he said, 'Here am I, my son.' He said, 'Behold, the fire and the wood, but where is the lamb for a burnt offering?' Abraham said, 'God will provide for Himself the lamb for a burnt offering, my son.' So they went both of them together. When they came to the place of which God had told him, Abraham built the altar there and laid the wood in order and bound Isaac his son and laid him on the altar, on top of the wood. Then Abraham reached out his hand and took the knife to slaughter his son." (Genesis 22:7-10 ESV)

Abraham's faith was strong, but what about Isaac's? The question that is put to Abraham must have torn at his heart. Is he alone in this? It is quite one thing for him to say that he was wholly committed to this course of action, but what about the one who was with him?

Isaac is probably not a small boy at this stage of his life. One commentator has put him in his early twenties. My perspective is that Isaac carried not only the physical DNA of his father, but also his spiritual DNA. Isaac trusted God, but it is obvious from the text that Abraham has not told him everything. They have the fire and the wood, but where is the sacrifice?

This is the pivotal point of the story. In verse 8, when Abraham utters incredible words of faith they do not easily slip off his tongue, but they come from a heart that has wrestled in the dark. That was enough for Isaac, who gathered his resolve and continued the journey with his father.

When they reach the summit of the mountain, Abraham builds the altar, puts the wood on it, binds and lays his son down and picks up the knife. At this point, his faith is probably the strongest it has ever been. Abraham knows that Isaac is the promised son and that in him lies a future filled with heaven's promise. He also knows that if he slays the boy God will resurrect him, because God has spoken to him, given him a covenant promise that reaches into the future, and God's promises are sure. Abraham is determined, knowing that both of them will go down the mountain in one piece. They will do it because within the boy is the promise of God.

The drama keeps unfolding. As Abraham prepares to plunge the knife into Isaac's chest, God speaks from heaven saying,

"Do not lay your hand on the boy or do anything to him, for now I know that you fear God, seeing you have not withheld your son, your only son, from Me." (Genesis 22:12 ESV)

Abraham had passed the test.

"And Abraham lifted up his eyes and looked, and behold, behind him was a ram, caught in a thicket by his horns. And Abraham went and took the ram and offered it up as a burnt offering instead of his son." (Genesis 22:13 ESV)

Here in this text there is a sense in the Hebrew rendering that God was saying, "Look behind you." Abraham turns around and there, right in front of him, is the provision of God. Paul Alexander, the principal of Mattersey Hall, gives the insightful thought that as father and son made their way up the mountain slope, God saw to it that a ram began to wander up on the other side.

Abraham slaughters the lamb and now begins to understand more of God's purposes that have to do with substitution. As a result of this, both of them come down the mountain. Verse 14 reads,

"So Abraham called the name of that place, 'The Lord will provide'; as it is said to this day, 'On the mount of the LORD it shall be provided.'" (Genesis 22:14 ESV)

The revelation

Throughout Abraham's journey and after his test comes the revelation. The meaning of "revelation" is to uncover what is already there, hidden from view. It's a peeling back of information to get to the heart of what is being said. In other words, it is the moment when "the spiritual penny drops".

Abraham calls the place YAHWEH JIREH: where God sees and provides. There is a very interesting play on words here, because the word "Moriah" means "chosen and seen of God". "Moriah" is the place where God's vision unfolds. God sees something in this place: He sees the need of Abraham and He provides. The beauty of this revelation is: God sees everything that we need before we need it.

Sometimes, when we consider God as Provider, we think of YAHWEH GIRO rather than YAHWEH JIREH! We think about money and we think about possessions and the stuff that we feel we need in our lives. This name of God assures us that He knows what we need, when we need it. God is a wonderful provider! How is it that we can have a need one Tuesday evening and a brown envelope containing all that we need comes through the letterbox on Wednesday morning? It happens because God saw our need before we had it and He arranged beforehand that the need and the provision would touch each other at exactly the right place and time.

I could tell you story after story of God's provision. When I was a member of a Christian band called "The Advocates" we used to be on the road quite a bit. There came a time when we needed some money to pay our collective bills – £236.84 to be exact. We got together and looked at what we needed to pay the bills and we realised this was a crisis moment for us. How were we going to find this money? We said to John, who was our treasurer, "Look in our joint bank account." John did so and discovered that we had £236.84 to the very penny! God saw our need ahead of us and He somehow put the money in our bank account – not a penny above and not a penny less.

There are times when there are a few more pennies on top because God tends to press His provision down, shake it together and make it run over! The point I am making is that whether it is in the realm of money or health or even in the realm of our future, God sees our need and He will provide. Whatever our need is at any particular time YAHWEH JIREH sees it. He sees it before we ever thought about it and He will help us.

Jesus was really strong on this. He told His disciples not to worry about tomorrow because God would take care of the tomorrows in their lives. The same goes for us. When we think of issues that will touch us in our future, we are encouraged not to worry because the God who is present with us now, is the God who is present there, and the need that we have then will be met by the God who sees the end from the beginning. He tells us not to be anxious because He will meet our every need. Paul, writes to the Philippians thus:

"And my God will meet all your needs according to his glorious riches in Christ Jesus." (Philippians 4:19 ESV)

Now if we stop here, we have a fantastic story. We have a father of faith and a restored son. But how is Isaac released? The answer is simple: a lamb took his place. God, in His sovereignty, saw to it that there would be a release for Isaac so that the promises of God could run to and through the nations – the result of which is that now when we sing "Father Abraham has many sons" we can count ourselves among them. We are the sons of Abraham because of the obedience of Abraham. We now walk in the fullness of that revelation.

The great and total fulfilment of this drama was worked out on another mount. The temple at Jerusalem was constructed on the site where Abraham and Isaac's story took place. And centuries later, on mount Calvary, another sacrifice took place nearby outside the city walls. The name of God, YAHWEH JIREH, the Lord who sees and provides, was enacted in fullness in the death of Christ. The question that was asked by Isaac, "Where is the lamb for the burnt offering?" was answered by John the Baptist:

"Behold the lamb of God who takes away the sin of the world." (John1:29 ESV)

It is the greatest story of all. Before the foundation of the world, God saw the dilemma of humanity and, at the right time, He sent His one and only Son to die on the cross so that we could be free. Just as Isaac was released, the amazing thing was that God did not hold back the judgement on His own Son, releasing Him to die on the cross. There was no one, no voice from heaven to say, "Stop!" Jesus became the perfect substitute, taking our sins upon His own body so that we could be fully forgiven, released and saved.

Jesus died in order that we might live. God saw our need before we did and He provided the answer in His Son. YAHWEH JIREH saw our sin, saw our loneliness, saw our sickness and saw our emptiness. He saw our heart, our pain, our lack and our fears. He saw our weakness, He saw our inadequacies, He heard our questions, noticed our poverty, our brokenness, our debt, our anger, our separation and, right when we needed it, He provided a Lamb. There is no better story in the whole world than this one. This is the good news: Jesus died so that we can live. He is our Saviour, Healer, Substitute, Lamb; He is our Deliverer and He is our Friend. He has paid the price.

Reflect and pray...

The call of God may require me to face some tough decisions, but He will never leave me. He leads me into blessing and fruitfulness.

Lord, you paid the ultimate price in order that I would know what it is to be really free. Sometimes I struggle with the truth that you are my provider, the One who sees everything about my life and my needs. It is easy to feel anxious about the future. I know that your Holy Spirit brings peace and assurance, so please fill me now. I want to live in freedom and walk joyfully into my destiny, so call me again into a life of devotion with you. Amen.

5
The Lord is my Peace

"All Scripture is breathed out by God." (2 Timothy 3:16 ESV)

God is a relational God. Every page of the Bible reveals the truths about His longing to connect with His people. Whenever there was a particular need, God would reveal Himself with a special name appropriate to that need in order to draw people to Himself. When His people needed a healer He would be YAHWEH RAPHAH – the Lord is your Healer. If they needed forgiveness He would be JEHOVAH MACCADDESHEM - the Lord who sanctifies.

In the 6th chapter of the book of Judges we find the story of the calling of Gideon. The people of Israel are in bondage yet again to their enemies and God is determined to deliver them from their oppression. The angel of the Lord makes an appearance to Gideon, who is in hiding, and tells him,

"The LORD is with you, mighty warrior." (Judges 6:12 NIV)

Gideon was not a man who had a positive self-image, so he found God's view of him as a mighty warrior at odds with how he saw himself. He questioned what was being said of him, asking God,

"Please, Lord, how can I save Israel? Behold, my clan is the weakest in Manasseh, and I am the least in my father's house." (Judges 6:15 ESV)

The word translated "weakest" is the Hebrew word, Dal which literally means, "to be left dangling through emaciation". Likewise, the word translated "least" is the Hebrew word Tsa`iyr meaning "little and insignificant". Gideon felt hopelessly inadequate and totally unable to face up to the challenge that God was laying at his feet. His primary need at this very moment, therefore, was for real encouragement and reassurance that God had somehow not picked the wrong man!

At this point, Gideon wanted to honour his heavenly visitor with a gift, so the angel agreed to wait.

"So Gideon went into his house and prepared a young goat and unleavened cakes from an ephah of flour. The meat he put in a basket, and the broth he put in a pot, and brought them to him under the terebinth and presented them. And the angel of God said to him, 'Take the meat and the unleavened cakes, and put them on this rock, and pour the broth over them.' And he did so. Then the angel of the LORD reached out the tip of the staff that was in his hand and touched the meat and the unleavened cakes. And fire sprang up from the rock and consumed the meat and the unleavened cakes. And the angel of the LORD vanished from his sight. Then Gideon perceived that he was the angel of the LORD." (Judges 6:19-22 ESV)

Gideon began to panic, as he knew that whenever people had a face-to-face encounter with the Lord, they usually died!

"'Alas, O Lord God! For now I have seen the angel of the Lord face to face.' But the LORD said to him, 'Peace be to you. Do not fear; you shall not die.' Then Gideon built an altar there to the Lord and called it, The Lord Is Peace." (Judges 6:22-24 ESV)

After such a radical encounter with God, Gideon was overcome with fear. Up to that point he had been secretly beating wheat in a winepress in order to hide it from the Midianites. He was just an ordinary man with an ordinary job minding his own business when one day an angel of God paid him a visit. It is very important that we do not lose the context of the story and how this must have felt to Gideon. It is not surprising that he talked to God about his inabilities and insecurities! By contrast, however, God's words to Gideon were powerful statements of affirmation and peace. Gideon would not die but live. We can almost feel the sense of relief that would have swept into Gideon's mind. Into a heart filled with turmoil and fear, the voice of God spoke and Gideon received a wonderful and fitting revelation of God as: YAHWEH SHALOM – the Lord is Peace.

The book of Judges is full of tales of the people of God. In it, we can read about the times they served Him, times of revival, of deliverance and freedom from their enemies, even times of separation when they forgot the Lord and turned from His ways. There are moving passages of repentance where the people of God sought the Lord and returned to Him, only to find that the whole cycle started over again. It is not that much different today!

It is in the middle of this that Gideon receives his revelation from God about who he himself is: a "mighty warrior". We rarely see ourselves as God sees us. Similarly, we often do not see God as He really is. Gideon encounters God not as a remote, frightening figure, but one who desires to be with him and bringing peace to him: YAHWEH SHARMA – the Lord is there and YAHWEH SHALOM – the Lord is Peace. In the middle of oppressive warfare, Gideon heard that the Lord was his peace. With all the threats and experiencing of wars across our world today, He says the same to us: "I am your Peace."

The biblical word "peace" is rich in texture and meaning. The Hebrew word for it, Shalom has a far wider and deeper sense of meaning than our English counterpart. In the Middle East, people use the word to

say "Hello" or to wish someone a nice day. But within it, the word
carries multiple nuances including completeness, soundness, wellbeing,
harmony, health, prosperity and safety. The International Standard
Encyclopaedia describes "Shalom" as "a condition of freedom from
disturbance, whether outwardly, as of a nation from war or enemies, or
inwardly, within the soul."

So God is "Shalom". God is peace and whenever He comes, He
comes with the reassurance that His presence will not cause fear or
stress or anxiety but a sense of calm and rest. This is a message that is
so vital for our world today and yet there was a day two thousand years
ago when the Prince of Peace stepped into our world and left a legacy
like no other. The apostle John recorded Jesus as having said,

"Peace I leave with you; my peace I give to you. Not as the world gives
do I give to you. Let not your hearts be troubled, neither let them be
afraid." (John.14:27 ESV)

He brings peace

Isaiah prophesied the coming of the Prince of Peace. Solomon, in one
of his two psalms, prayed prophetically about the Messiah thus:

"In his days may the righteous flourish, and peace abound, till the
moon be no more!" (Psalm72:7 ESV)

In that great passage in Isaiah chapter 9:6, we read,

"For to us a child is born, to us a son is given; and the government
shall be upon his shoulder, and his name shall be called Wonderful
Counsellor, Mighty God, Everlasting Father, Prince of Peace." (Isaiah
9:6 ESV)

In the opening chapters of his gospel, Luke brilliantly captures an atmosphere of expectation. People are waiting for something, for someone. In the Temple area, there were three elderly people, Zechariah, Simeon and Anna, who were waiting for the promised Messiah to come, longing for His appearance. If we had have been there, we would have almost felt it in the air as a yearning or a longing. The people of God had been waiting for centuries for a Messiah, but at that particular time the sense of expectancy was heightened. It was not just felt by the devout Jews but by everyone. Three Roman historians speak of it. Tacitus wrote, "Many were persuaded that it was contained in the ancient books of their priests, that at that time, the East should prevail, and that someone should proceed from Judea and possess the dominion." Suetonius, writing on the life of Vespasian, wrote, "An ancient and settled persuasion prevailed throughout the East, that the Fates had decreed someone to proceed from Judea who should attain universal empire." Josephus, the secular Jewish historian, wrote in a similar vein.

Zachariah prophesied over his miracle infant son, John. He said,

"And you, child, will be called the prophet of the Most High; for you will go before the Lord to prepare His ways, to give knowledge of salvation to His people in the forgiveness of their sins, because of the tender mercy of our God, whereby the sunrise shall visit us from on high to give light to those who sit in darkness and in the shadow of death, to guide our feet into the way of peace." (Luke1: 76-79 ESV)

The coming one was to guide us into the paths of peace, into the path of "Shalom". The same God who revealed Himself as YAHWEH SHALOM to Gideon is exactly the same God who wants to lead us today into a pathway of peace. This is His heart.

In this same passage of Luke, Simeon, an old man who had been promised that before he closed his eyes in death he would see for himself the promised Messiah, took the infant Jesus in his arms, praising God saying,

"Lord, now you are letting your servant depart in peace, according to your word; for my eyes have seen your salvation that you have prepared in the presence of all peoples, a light for revelation to the Gentiles, and for glory to your people Israel." (Luke 2:29-32 ESV)

This old prophet had been waiting, but now the Messiah was in his arms and he was at peace.

In the midst of the pressures of life today, surrounded by global events that are dark and threatening, we cry out for a visitation of God, knowing that when His presence comes it brings a peace that the world cannot understand. His peace is deeper than just a feeling – it seeps into our troubled souls, keeping us steady and strong while everything around us is turbulent.

Peace has come into our dark, war-torn world. Peace continues to be poured into it from heaven, moment by moment and, of course, Isaiah 9 speaks prophetically of the Prince of Peace one who is to come:

"For to us a child is born, to us a Son is given; and the government shall be upon His shoulder, and his name shall be called Wonderful Counsellor, Mighty God, Everlasting Father, Prince of Peace. Of the increase of His government and of peace there will be no end, on the throne of David and over his kingdom, to establish it and to uphold it with justice and with righteousness from this time forth and forevermore. The zeal of the LORD of hosts will do this." (Isaiah 9:6-7 ESV)

Reflect and pray...

Peace that comes from God is not a feeling or a state of mind. It is heart to heart, spirit to spirit.

Lord, I am deeply grateful for your peace that sustains me through times of stress and fear. You are so good at calming the storms by saying "Peace, be still." I want my life to reflect your name, YAHWEH SHALOM. so that people around me can learn about you in and through me. Amen.

6
The Lord is my Healer

In this chapter we look at an incident recorded in Exodus chapter 15:22-26. In the wilderness of Shur at a place called Marah the thirsty Israelites could only find bitter water and they started to complain about their leader Moses. Moses in turn took this issue to the Lord, who gave him a solution .

"The Lord showed him a log, and he threw it into the water, and the water became sweet." (Exodus 15:25 ESV)

God then gave Moses a fresh revelation, saying,

"If you will diligently listen to the voice of the Lord your God, and do that which is right in His eyes, and give ear to His commandments and keep all His statutes, I will put none of the diseases on you that I put on the Egyptians, for I am the Lord, your healer." (Exodus 15:26 ESV)

YAHWEH RAPHAH – the Lord is my Healer

We know that God is not confined to one name. As we read through the Scriptures, we see an unfolding revelation of the greatness and goodness of the God who reveals aspects of His nature and character through every one of His names.

The Hebrew word Raphah can be translated "one who heals"

"physician" or "doctor". It is comforting to know that as we come to God with our needs, we find that He is our Great Physician who will never make us wait for an appointment! "YAHWEH RAPHAH" restores people to full health and vitality in line with His perfect plan and design for creation.

In order to fully understand this truth, it is important to set it in the context in which it was written. Exodus 15 is a chapter containing a lot of water! In verse 22, we read that,

"Moses made Israel set out from the Red Sea."

It was impossible for a nation of men, women, children and livestock to cross the Red Sea safely since it was much too wide and the water far too deep. It needed a sovereign and powerful work of God to divide it so that the Israelites had safe passage.

As they passed through, with a wall of water either side of them, these walls symbolised walls of opposition which had become walls of opportunity. Leaving Egypt, a place of oppression and slavery for a land full of promise was all part of God's plan to heal and establish the nation of Israel.

In the same verse we read that the Israelites "went into the wilderness of Shur." The word, "Shur" means "wall". It is almost as if, after passing through the Red Sea, they encountered another wall, only this time it was not made of water. Reaching their next destination, Marah (meaning "bitter") they do find water, but it is completely undrinkable. So their journey progressed through too much water, no water and finally undrinkable water.

What is happening here? I believe that the Lord was allowing the Israelites to go through a season of testing. For quite some time, both in Egypt and out if it, they had been experiencing the power of God in many different ways. Whether it was through the humiliation of

Pharaoh and the gods of Egypt by the nine plagues, the leading of God in the pillar of fire and the cloud, or the division of the Red Sea and the total destruction of the Egyptian army as the waters rolled back, God was intervening supernaturally in their lives on a regular basis.

At this point in Exodus things were starting to go wrong and it looked like the favour of the Lord had been taken away. Perhaps if you or I would have witnessed such miraculous activity in and around us, we would have been changed forever and never doubt the closeness of God's presence, but the Israelites instead began to moan and complain. The Bible refers to them as "grumbling" for the first time – and it will certainly not be the last!

God was not just leading the Israelites into a new place geographically, but also into a new place of maturity. He wanted His people to move from an experience- based walk to a faith-filled walk. In order for this to happen, they were exposed to situations that would challenge their expectations. It is a view held by many that whilst the easy times are pleasant, it is in the difficult times of life that we learn and grow.

It is quite possible to have a powerful conversion experience where, like the Israelites, we come out of the bondage of Egypt into a place of freedom and deliverance. We can live off those moments of divine intervention for years, with vivid memories of the power of God, knowing that He is a God to be feared, honoured and respected.

Similar to our miracle of salvation and the release from oppression, the Israelites had experienced a powerful event as they left Egypt and crossed the Red Sea. In the same way that after conversion God works, with our permission, to change us from the inside out, the people of God were about to learn that God was able to restore them, to put them back together and to heal them. They had come out of Egypt, but a lot of Egypt was still in them.

The journey from Egypt to Canaan

After leaving Egypt, the final destination for the Israelites was, of course, Canaan – the Promised Land. I have heard some preachers draw parallels saying that the Promised Land is a picture of heaven, but I believe this is misguided.

The Promised Land is our inheritance whilst we are yet still on the earth. We do not get saved and then wait around until heaven calls. There is too much to be done in us, through us and for us in this life before we reach the next.

The first part of their journey was actually coming out of Egypt, a land where they had been for many years as slaves to foreign rulers. When they came to the Red Sea, not only was God going to bring them out of Egypt, He was going to deliver them from Pharaoh's power and authority once and for all. The liberation of God is comprehensive in nature. To really break out of Egypt, the people had to break through and pass through the Red Sea, and that experience was a forerunner of the rite of baptism.

When we get baptized we are saying "no" to the old life and "yes" to the new one. When the pursuing Egyptian army was wiped out as the waters came crashing back, so God wants to set us free from the powers of sin and darkness, destroying their hold on us forever.

They had come through the waters, arriving at some more water in Marah that should have been a source of life and refreshment, and it was here that the God revealed another of His names: YAHWEH RAPHAH – the Lord is your Healer.

"There the LORD made for them a statute and a rule, and there he tested them, saying, 'If you will diligently listen to the voice of the LORD your God, and do that which is right in his eyes, and give ear to his commandments and keep all his statutes, I will put none of the diseases on you that I put on the Egyptians, for I am the LORD your healer.'" (Exodus 15:25-26 ESV)

It is important that we see that it is possible to be saved, but not whole. It is possible to have our sins forgiven and be on our way to heaven, but still struggle with our past. God does not want us to mark time until we get to heaven, He wants to bring restoration and healing into our "Egypt-filled" lives. He wants us to experience the power of liberation from our old ways, our old regime, and the power of sin and darkness.

This is why baptism is so important. Baptism is a declaration that the old life has gone and that a new one has begun. When we descend under the water, it is a symbol of the burial of the old life and a deep identification with the death and burial of Christ. As we are brought through waters, we are stating that the old has passed, that everything is being renewed and we find ourselves moving into the land God has promised us. On this new journey there is healing to be found at the deepest level.

While it is important, God's plan for our lives extends far beyond making us morally clean: He is intent on our complete wholeness, body, mind, emotions and spirit. After baptism, our journey continues into an encounter with YAHWEH RAPHAH – the Lord our Healer. Many of us have been saved and baptized and yet we still carry "baggage" from our past, from things that have happened to us or been spoken over us which have wounded us. So too, we can be bound by guilt over choices we have made that have inflicted pain on others.

In 1 Thessalonians Paul writes,

"Now may the God of peace himself sanctify you completely, and may your whole spirit and soul and body be kept blameless at the coming of our Lord Jesus Christ." (1 Thessalonians 5:23 ESV)

The words "to heal" are multi-faceted and I have chosen three definitions in an attempt to convey in just how many contexts they can be used:

First, "to heal" is "to mend as a garment is mended". Second it means "to repair as a building is repaired and reconstructed" and thirdly, it means "to cure as a diseased person is restored to health".

God wants to heal us in every dimension of our lives. He wants to deal with the baggage of our past sins and He wants us to come under the righteousness that is ours in God. He wants us to live differently and to think differently. He will renew our minds – the way we think, which will in turn affect the way we act, the way we respond and the way we interact with people.

God revives the spirit

The moment we trust in Christ, our spirit wakes up. We know that if we were to die at that very moment we would be welcomed in heaven. The spirit that has previously been locked up is unlocked through repentance and the door is opened to a living relationship with God. There are many who have lived evil lives who can say that in that moment in time when they trusted Christ, everything changed and light flooded in. Even the colours of nature became sharper and more defined.

God restores the soul

Returning to the 23rd Psalm we read how the Lord, who is our Shepherd, "restores our soul". What does that mean? I believe it means that He pours healing and loving revelation into the realms of our emotions or thought patterns and our will, changing us from the inside out to be more like Him. With our permission, His Spirit inhabits those areas of our lives which have been hurt, damaged or locked up. God wants to heal in these areas, making us whole again.

God rejuvenates the body

The word "rejuvenate" means "to give new youth to". The work of God in our lives helps us to come to a place where we begin to feel a lightness coming into our spirit and soul. I have to be careful with this because "looking younger" is not the issue here! The life of God, resident in us by the Holy Spirit, is eternal in nature, so even as our body ages, our inner life is renewed. Remember the words of David about the righteous who,

"...still bear fruit in old age; they are ever full of sap and green..." (Psalm 92:14 ESV)

Despite the aging process, these people remain tender hearted, flexible and still growing and producing. Not only do they grow old with dignity, they grow old full of life!

What is the will of God?

We know that if YAHWEH RAPHAH – the Lord is your Healer, is one of the names of God, then by definition He is against sickness and for health. Whilst we know that sickness is part of the world in which we live, it is vital that we continue to lay hold of this truth from Scripture to help us as we pray. We are encouraged to have a foundation of faith in our God as Healer. From this foundation we can pray in faith for the situations we face for which we have no answers. Sickness will never come from God – He is all good and when He designed us there was no flaw in the process and plan; no room given for infirmity. When sin entered His world, it brought sickness with it, so we acknowledge its place here, but we do not accept that it is part of God's heart for us.

Imagine driving your car along the motorway when suddenly the red warning light comes on and you realise that there is a problem. It may need oil or water or there may be something more serious that needs your attention. The obvious thing to do is either to pull in and top up the oil or water or take it in to a mechanic and get it looked at. It is the same with us. If we are to "run smoothly" and in full health, we need to be alert and take measures to maintain health and wholeness.

Sometimes, however, sickness comes to the healthiest of people for no apparent reason. It is so important in those times that we do not lose the foundational truth that God is a good God who will never cause anyone to be ill or to die before their time. His heart aches when His people suffer.

You may know our story about when our son David had cancer and, as a family, we stared death in the face. In this and many other times, we can testify to the supernatural power of God who has healed us. Some of you reading these words will have been touched by similar things, so let me encourage you to continue to proclaim God as your Healer. He comes through for His people time and time again, both suddenly and miraculously, and also by using the skills of the surgeons and doctors. Bad theology that says God is anything other than good robs us of the faith to press in for healing. I am incredulous that many churches do not talk about or preach on healing, and yet all the way through the pages of Scripture, from Genesis to Revelation, there is ample and clear evidence of healings and miracles. His name is Healer: so believe it!

You may have noticed that in the Exodus passage we are considering, there are conditional clauses to the promise of healing where the word "if" is mentioned. In effect, God is saying to the people of Israel, "If you diligently listen to my voice; if you do that which is right in my eyes; if you give ear to my commandments and keep my statutes, then I will fulfil the promise of healing." This was a covenant of healing made between two parties: God and the children of Israel and their healing was dependent upon their obedience.

Many read this passage and immediately count themselves out of being healed, feeling that as their personal obedience falls short of what is required, God will not make them better. But remember, this is how it all operated in the Old Testament under the old covenant. As we move into the New Testament there is a new covenant and it is of a different order.

Healing is central to the gospel and the ministry of Jesus demonstrated the power of the kingdom of God as He travelled from town to town. God had not changed, His covenant remained intact, but the huge difference was that Jesus fulfilled all the requirements of the old covenant while bringing in the new. The promise is now held out to us because of and through the obedience of Christ. It is not dependent on how good we are or how much we pray, it is dependent upon the finished work of Christ, Immanuel, God with us. In a real sense God has fulfilled His own requirements and the promise is made manifest through simple childlike faith and trust. If we are able to receive this then we will walk into more and more health, life and wholeness. If, as churches, we begin to teach and proclaim it, I believe we will see more of the kingdom of God among us and many more healings. The late John Wimber once made a simple, yet profound comment:

"Those who pray for healing see more people healed than those who don't."

Under the old covenant God knew that although He was dependable and would keep His side of the covenant, the people were not as faithful. In Exodus 15:22-26 the people were grumbling because they had come to the waters of Marah and found them bitter. Grumbling always erupts from the seedbed of unbelief and mistrust and turns the atmosphere into an attraction for sickness. The medical profession will tell us that heart and mental attitudes of resentment and bitterness can affect our health. Such occurrences are called psychosomatic symptoms, where the issues of the mind (psyche) affect the issues of the body (soma).

How we approach God is very important. If we are grumbling and carrying resentment and bitterness in our hearts, we can become a prime target for sickness. But if we are able to release people by forgiveness, cutting them loose from any blame that we would hold against them, if we are able to say that we want to be right with God and right with other people, then we put ourselves in the position of being able to receive healing. Paul writes,

"Whoever, therefore, eats the bread or drinks the cup of the Lord in an unworthy manner will be guilty concerning the body and blood of the Lord. Let a person examine himself, then, and so eat of the bread and drink of the cup. For anyone who eats and drinks without discerning the body eats and drinks judgment on himself. That is why many of you are weak and ill, and some have died." (1 Corinthians 11:27-30 ESV)

This means that when we do not recognise and discern the body (meaning those believers around us) we make ourselves open and vulnerable to judgement. When we take communion, we need to be clean.

The converse, then, must be true. If we approach the table in a worthy manner, discerning and recognising those around us, then the healing and restorative virtue of Christ can flow into our lives.

Healing in the Bible

Throughout the Old Testament there are many accounts of healing, especially by the prophets Elijah and Elisha. Under their ministry we read of some pretty dramatic and visible healings where the dead were raised, lepers were cleansed and the sick were healed.

Of course, Jesus is the greatest example of them all. He healed every kind of disease and sickness. Nothing was too difficult to heal. Matthew records that,

"Great crowds came to Him, bringing with them the lame, the blind, the crippled, the mute, and many others, and they put them at His feet, and He healed them, so that the crowd wondered, when they saw the mute speaking, the crippled healthy, the lame walking, and the blind seeing. And they glorified the God of Israel." (Matthew 15: 30-31 ESV)

If we were to take the miraculous out of the gospels, we would have very little content left, simply because wherever Jesus went, miracles took place. Even when Jesus turns away from preaching and teaching the multitudes and spends time in prayer on the mountain, when He returns to them, He finds that,

"...the power of the Lord was with Him to heal." (Luke 5:17 ESV)

After Pentecost, the early Church witnessed the healing of the sick and the raising of the dead as normal occurrences. The Spirit that had been with Jesus was now with ordinary men, women and children through whom many miracles were activated. The New Testament is full of stories of miraculous healings, expulsions of demons and resurrections. It all makes for exciting reading! This is the God we love and serve:

YAHWEH RAPHAH – the Lord our Healer.

The end of the New Testament does not mark the end of the miraculous. All through the centuries that have followed there has been a consistent witness to the supernatural working of the Holy Spirit, especially in terms of healing. Many of the early Church fathers testified to miraculous healings taking place through their ministries, changing the world around them for the glory of God. Over the last few centuries, however, this light has grown dim and the Enlightenment brought a severe challenge to the whole concept of the supernatural working of God. So too, liberal biblical scholars have systematically challenged the veracity of the supernatural, stating that all these things ceased upon the death of the apostles. This doctrine is called "cessationism". The case made is that the miraculous was needed to establish the Church in such antagonistic circumstances, but now that the Word of God has come, there is no further need of the supernatural. As the basis of their argument they use 1 Corinthians 13:9-10:

"For we know in part and we prophesy in part, but when the perfect comes, the partial will pass away." (ESV)

Unfortunately, this is a gross misunderstanding of the text. The cessationist view that the "perfect" is the canon of Scripture is at odds with the truth which is a reference to the coming of Christ. Thankfully, over the last 30 years there has been a substantial restoration of the supernatural to the Church and miracles are exploding everywhere!

God's healing has always been a topic of controversy and sadly a lot of the challenge has come from within the Church itself. Liberal and unbelieving theology has robbed believers of the truth concerning the goodness of God. For example, the whole principle of water baptism is clear: that choosing to be baptized and coming through the waters is moving from death to life, from an old way of living to a new one, stepping into the resurrection life of Christ which is characterized by the filling of the Holy Spirit. However, when there was a shift from believer's baptism to infant baptism, something was missing. Newborn babies are unable to confess Christ themselves, nor could they desire to be filled with the Holy Spirit. Praise God for the Baptists and Anabaptists who kept baptism alive, insisting that it was for believers, severing us from the past and introducing us into a new way of living.

Throughout history there have been various Church movements that have worked against the healing ministry. I want to pinpoint some of them.

Extreme ascetism

This over-zealous devotion to monastic rules and severe abstinence was characterized in its extreme form by pushing people into a belief system that the body itself was evil and focusing only on the spiritual nature was important in order to get into heaven. The physical life, including sexual relationships within marriage, was considered evil. This resulted in the elevation of physical suffering as a virtue in order to please the Lord, who could only be interested in the spiritual part of man. People would actually take great comfort and feel intensely spiritual if they were suffering for the Lord.

The use of "ascetic" is misleading as a title, however. Rather than "emaciated, harsh and a hater of pleasure" with which it has come to be associated, the Oxford Dictionary actually defines it, "severely abstinent or austere". It comes from the Greek word Askesis which simply means "exercise". In its fullest sense, it meant "training for" or "exercise in excellence" and implies years of disciplined and repetitive behaviour in order to improve.

We are created in the image of God and our physical nature is made to be whole and well, just as is the case with our spiritual nature. The violent and negative dogma of the extreme ascetics is not in line with God's view of mankind, since He cares about our bodies and wants them to be prosperous and healthy.

We all love the bursts of spontaneous brilliance that can come from a quality musician, but behind such flashes is a history of daily, repetitive, often boring rehearsing, exercises and training. We love to see brilliant performances on the sports field, but as Dallas Willard points out,

"The star performer himself didn't achieve his excellence by trying to behave in a certain way only during the game. Instead he chose an overall life of preparation of mind and body, pouring all his energies into that total preparation, to provide a foundation in the body's automatic responses and strength for his conscious efforts during the game … it is a daily regimen that no one sees."

In reality, we all need to develop a personal askesis. To use other helpful analogies, this can be seen as the "cultivating of a garden", the "shaping of a soul", the "training of a soldier". It is all about the driving down of deep roots into the life of God. Here, I am thinking about building for the future, as opposed to living constantly in the immediate. I believe what God is looking for in us is well-built, strong, mature Christians who will be strong in their faith, passionate for Christ and "influencers" for the kingdom in years to come.

Jesus suffered for all of mankind. His work on the cross was unique and never to be repeated by anyone. As the prophet Isaiah put it,

"Surely He has borne our griefs and carried our sorrows; yet we esteemed Him stricken, smitten by God, and afflicted. But He was wounded for our transgressions; He was crushed for our iniquities;

upon Him was the chastisement that brought us peace, and with His stripes we are healed." (Isaiah 53:4-5 ESV)

Please don't misunderstand me. There are people who have suffered greatly and God has used that process in their life for great and wonderful things. But extreme ascetism (as opposed to healthy ascetism) says that we become really holy by punishing and denying our body in order to win the friendship and blessing of God. During the early years of Church history there were poor individuals who sat for years on top of pillars, hid themselves away in caves and even mutilated themselves for the sake of the kingdom. This religious philosophy infiltrated the life of the Church with devastating consequences. Sickness and pain had become a virtue. All this is miles away from the truth.

Elitism

Another challenge to the truth that God is and always has been YAHWEH RAPHAH is that only really spiritual people have the supernatural gifts of the Spirit. In Church history this explained the process of the veneration of the saints. This stream of religious thought believed that only really special saints were imbued with special powers for healing and other such gifts. These gifts were not accessible to ordinary people and healing was confined to special people and special places. Pilgrimages to venues with healing waters or where there had been visions of Mary were deemed spiritual and desirable.

So the healing ministry, which was meant to be in the hands of ordinary men and women, was now on platforms and in special places and administered by special "anointed" people. However, Scripture is clear that we are all saints. John Wimber taught that, "the healing ministry is meant to be manifest in the pews." This ministry is meant to be in the hands of us all, not just in the hands of the specialists!

You may not be aware that for about 700 years in England and France, only the monarch was seen as the one who could administer healing. It was the right of monarchs and was called the "royal touch". On special occasions they would pray for sick people and because God is gracious and always wants to heal, people would actually recover!

There were a vast number of ungodly monarchs, but because of their divine right as kings and their position in the land, they were able actually to pray for the sick and people would get well. We can see how far we are from where God intended us to be. Because we have swallowed the lie that we have to be a special person in a special place, we feel that we are disqualified from ever believing that God could use ordinary people like us to heal the sick. It is my belief that these things have been systematically working in the Church against the true purposes of God.

Liberalism

There is a lot that I could write about this, but I simply want to say that for many years Western theologians have written that the wonder of the miraculous is nothing but myth and superstition. The commentaries are not all bad; many of them have material that is very helpful to our understanding of certain truths. But as they do not endorse the supernatural it has become a belief system that has filtered into our culture and been sown into our churches. Liberalism will present Jesus as just a wonderful moral teacher, but with no power and no authority.

Dispensationalism

This particular thread of Christian teaching separated history into epochs or eras hence the name dispensational theology. Miracles and supernatural healings were placed in the apostolic era, meaning that belief in miracles at any other time is unnecessary and irrelevant. At some point, there will come another epoch or dispensation when the miracles will return, and that will be in the Millennium – the thousand-year rule of Christ on the earth. Some Bibles, such as the Schofield and Derby Bible, even have this teaching in their footnotes.

God never intended epochs and dispensations whereby His acts would be put in little time boxes. His intention has always been that ordinary people, throughout the ages, expressing faith in Jesus, would see healings and miracles released among them.

Secularism

The Enlightenment brought with it an elevating of reason above God. Concepts that could not be reasoned through logically were rejected as myths and strange stories. In secularism, only what could be seen and touched was of any importance; the spiritual world was merely a figment of the foolish imagination. Nevertheless, secularism has insidiously and deliberately infiltrated our society through our education systems and the media, challenging the value of faith in what is unseen.

By His stripes

Supernatural healing has been challenged throughout Church history. If you want to discover more about the truth of this, I would heartily recommend an excellent book by a Roman Catholic scholar called Francis McNutt. It is called, The Nearly Perfect Crime: How the Church almost killed the ministry of healing. Just as God's intention in our lives is wholeness, the enemy has also had a strategy and a plan – that is to kill, steal and destroy (John 10:10). If the saints will believe that the testimonies of miracles are simply fanciful story telling and mythology, we will never see the kingdom of God come in fullness. We must break out of these harmful historical mindsets, these dusty denominational traditions that oppose the work of the Spirit. We have to start believing again that the normal Christian life is coming out of Egypt, coming away from the bondages of the past and the rule of Satan, getting baptized, shaking off the old way of living, coming into a sweet wholeness, getting baptized in the Holy Spirit and operating in His power. This is where the fun begins; this is where real life begins; this is where heaven comes down!

Healing is found in one Name and one Name only: YAHWEH RAPHAH – the Lord is our Healer. Into a context of a grumbling people who should have known better, Scripture says that Moses,

"...cried to the Lord, and the Lord showed him a log." (Exodus15:25 ESV)

In the Hebrew language the word "showed" is Yarah. That is the root word from which we get Torah, which means "law" or "teaching". As Moses cried out to God, the Lord taught him something. He taught him that if he took this particular piece of wood and introduced it into the waters of bitterness that healing would come. What a wonderful allegory of the cross of Christ. The Bible teaches us that there was a piece of wood destined to carry the weight of Jesus the Son of God, and as that sacrifice was dipped into the bitter suffering and sickness of this world, a healing wave was released. It is by His stripes we are healed.

In addition, we have been given authority to say, "In the name of Jesus Christ of Nazareth be made whole." He has given us His Name, above every other name, to speak healing and release. This authority is not based on our own inherent goodness, nor is it purely resident in certain powerful healing evangelists; it is based completely in the finished work of Jesus Christ. He is our righteousness, He is our healer and He is our strong deliverer. Hallelujah!

When it comes to the healing ministry, we should all be involved. It is part of our birth right. I believe that we are being invited to rise to new levels of faith, reaching into God for the power and the gifts of the Holy Spirit, and reaching out to the sick and the suffering around us. We have to learn again to take authority in our homes, with our children, with the various situations that occur in and around us. We have been given a wonderful Name – the Name of Jesus – the same one who is YAHWEH RAPHAH – the Lord our Healer. Let's use it!

Reflect and pray...

God, through Jesus, has paid the price on the cross for my healing and wholeness.

Lord, when I gave my life to you, I gave you permission to unlock my heart and fill me with your love and mercy. Nothing is hidden from you: nothing I have done and nothing that has been done to me. I will trust you to highlight the areas in my life that need your healing touch and I submit myself to your kindness and care. You are my Healer, body, mind and soul, and so I lay hold now of my inheritance in you and invite you to change me. Amen.

7
The Lord is my Saviour

So far we have understood from the Old Testament how the name of God was so holy, so intimate, that Israelites would revere it, not letting it so much as cross their lips. This covenant-keeping God, YAHWEH, was always there to love, defend, discipline and bless His people and He is the same yesterday, today and forever.

In this chapter, I want to venture into the New Testament, pulling all the great names of God together into one great Name. The name of Jesus captures the very heartbeat of God our Father: Jesus is YAHWEH, "our Salvation". The name "Jesus" actually appears over 600 times in the gospels and the Greek rendering IESOUS literally means "YAHWEH is Salvation".

The word from the angel of the Lord that came to Joseph the artisan was,

"Joseph, son of David, do not fear to take Mary as your wife, for that which is conceived in her is from the Holy Spirit. She will bear a son, and you shall call his name Jesus, for he will save his people from their sins." (Matthew 1:20-21 ESV)

The story running through the whole Bible, both Old and New Testaments, is the unfolding revelation of Christ, who became the "Word made flesh" (John 1) – God incarnate among us. He is the heartbeat of God expressed in the God-man Jesus Christ. The writer to the Hebrews tells us that Jesus,

"…is the radiance of the glory of God and the exact imprint of his nature…" (Hebrews 1:3 ESV)

Paul tells us that,

"He is the image of the invisible God…" (Colossians 1:15 ESV)

And that we see,

"…the glory of God in the face of Jesus Christ." (2 Corinthians 4:6 ESV)

In certain parts of the world, such as South America, the name "Jesus" is very common. It is not unusual to hear it spoken often within communities and families whose sons have grown up identified with it. However, it is this name, above all other names, that sums up and carries within it the heartbeat of God. When combined with "Christ", meaning "anointed", it becomes even more so, conveying the essence of who God is and what He came to do: the anointed Saviour, Jesus Christ.

The Old Testament rendition of "Jesus" is "Joshua" or "Jehoshua". The wonderful thing about reading the whole Bible is that we begin to see the plans and purposes of God to redeem mankind. Throughout the Old Testament we get glimpses of what God is like and everything points to Jesus. In fact, when Jesus met the two disciples trudging back home to Emmaus from Jerusalem after the crucifixion, Luke writes,

"And beginning with Moses and all the Prophets, He interpreted to them in all the Scriptures the things concerning Himself." (Luke 24:27 ESV)

Later, when Jesus was with the disciples in Jerusalem, He encouraged them by telling them that,

"...everything written about Me in the Law of Moses and the Prophets and the Psalms must be fulfilled." (Luke 24:44 ESV)

There are three key elements of the name of Jesus and my hope is that as you read the following, you will encounter fresh revelation of what His name means for you.

A saving name

The first thing is that the name "Jesus" is a saving name. When the angel appeared to Mary with the instruction to call her baby "Jesus" it was not just a random choice – a name picked out of the air or from an old baby book. This baby was the Son of God and by naming Him Jesus, God was communicating to His world that it needed saving and He was the Saviour.

When the angel appeared to Joseph in a dream, the meaning of the name "Jesus" was doubly emphasised:

"Joseph, son of David, do not fear to take Mary as your wife, for that which is conceived in her is from the Holy Spirit. She will bear a Son, and you shall call His name Jesus, for He will save His people from their sins." (Matthew 1:20-21 ESV)

Mary and Joseph were left in no doubt that their child was special, both in the way He was conceived and what His life would mean. God had named their child and given them the responsibility of raising Him into adulthood.

We have already seen the similarities between the Hebrew and

Greek rendering of the names "Jesus" and "Joshua", and in the Old Testament there are two significant men called "Joshua" who point the way for the Jesus who is to come. One was the servant of Moses, who eventually took on the leadership of the nation of Israel leading them into the Promised Land and the other was a high priest in the days of Ezra and Nehemiah.

The first Joshua was with Moses when the Israelites were delivered out of Egypt. He was there when a whole nation was set free from bondage. He saw the waters of the Red Sea part at God's instruction. He was there when the bitter waters at Marah became sweet. When Moses died, Joshua led the people to their permanent home where they could settle and raise their families in safety, peace and fruitfulness. This is a wonderful picture of the New Testament Jesus who brought us out of the bondage of sin into the promised land of God's blessing and provision. He takes us out and away from what we were and He takes us into all that we shall become. In this sense, Joshua is an Old Testament picture of a saviour – a foretaste of the coming Messiah.

The second Joshua is found in the account from the days of Ezra and Nehemiah. He was a High Priest in the temple and was instrumental in leading the people of God out of their Babylonian exile and back to Jerusalem.

We read in Hebrews that Jesus is also our great High Priest.

"Now the point in what we are saying is this: we have such a high priest, one who is seated at the right hand of the throne of the Majesty in heaven." (Hebrews 8:1 ESV)

Joshua is also involved in the rebuilding of the Temple. Once again, this is a powerful parallel to Jesus the Messiah who one day would deliver people out of their Babylon, out of hopelessness and emptiness, returning them back home to Jerusalem, the city of God. In that place

He would build a "temple" not made with human hands, but with living stones and it would be called the Church. Peter the Apostle would write to believers that,

"You yourselves like living stones are being built up as a spiritual house, to be a holy priesthood, to offer spiritual sacrifices acceptable to God through Jesus Christ." (1 Peter 2:5 ESV)

Paul echoes these words:

"The household of God, built on the foundation of the Apostles and Prophets, Christ Jesus Himself being the cornerstone, in whom the whole structure, being joined together, grows into a holy temple in the Lord. In Him you also are being built together into a dwelling place for God by the Spirit." (Ephesians 2:19-22 ESV)

In the Psalms we read,

"O Israel, hope in the Lord! For with the Lord there is steadfast love, and with Him is plentiful redemption. And He will redeem Israel from all his iniquities." (Psalm 130:7-8 ESV)

These words carry the same theme of redemption. Notice the phrase is almost identical to the words that the angel brought to Mary:

"He will save His people from their sins." (Matthew 1:21 ESV)

I want to ask you, the reader, are you saved? Have you come to know Jesus personally as your own Saviour, Friend and Lord? I will guarantee that when you find Him, you find life in all its fullness. In the same way that Joshua, the servant of Moses led the people out of captivity and into the Promised Land, Jesus can bring you out of the deathly emptiness of a life without God and into a relationship with your Heavenly Father.

It can be easy to not understand fully what it means to be saved and focus on the negative side in the sense of being saved from sin and from death. It is true that we are saved from those things, but there is much more to it than that! We are also saved into God and saved into eternal life. The central theme is both being saved from sin and being brought into a new realm of living. In addition, we have learned that God is not just interested in our souls, He is interested in every part of who we are. We are saved from sin, yes, but also saved from physical dangers, sickness, disease and the power of death itself.

Peter, answering the Sanhedrin, said to them,

"This Jesus is the stone that was rejected by you, the builders, which has become the cornerstone. And there is salvation in no one else, for there is no other Name under heaven given among men by which we must be saved." (Acts 4:11-12 ESV)

We live in an extremely pluralistic society that reveres and respects many differing points of view. One of the most popular systems of belief today is that there are a number of roads that lead to God. As Christians we believe that there are many roads to finding the answer, but there is only one answer, only one way to God: Jesus. Jesus, Himself said to Thomas the disciple when he asked how they could know the way,

"I am the way, and the truth, and the life. No one comes to the Father except through me." (John14:6 ESV)

Jesus did not say He was "a way," but "the way." He did not say He was "a version of the truth" but "the truth."

The Bible clearly states there is only one Name given for the salvation of mankind and that is the Name of Jesus. There is only one Saviour who is good enough and only one Saviour who has paid the price on the cross to set us free. He has taken our sin upon Himself, carrying our burdens, so that when we believe in Him we will have everlasting life. There is no other gospel; there is no other Way; there is no other Truth; there is no other Life.

A dynamic name

Not only is the name of Jesus a saving name, it is also a dynamic name, as relevant today as it ever was. Some great and influential names may come to mind when we consider significant seasons or events in history, but their names do not live! They are confined to the past, perhaps leaving a legacy of their work in books or art or music and so on, but nevertheless they remain just a memory. The name of Jesus is not like that.

The word "dynamic" means "energy" or "a force that produces motion". Each time today the name of Jesus is spoken there is a dynamic movement that takes place, because Jesus is alive today. His Name is as active and vibrant as it ever was, resonating throughout the universe for all of creation to hear, but also wonderfully intimate and personal for the individual. YAHWEH, the great "I AM", is not locked up in history in some irrelevant biography – He is alive!

When we trace the life of the early Church, particularly through the Acts of the Apostles and also in part of the gospels, we find that when the disciples were commissioned by Jesus He gave them permission to use His name. As they went out they began to use the name of Jesus with startling effects. Miracles were released among the people. The wonderful thing is that God has given us the ability to use the name of Jesus and that His name carries power.

So often, when we pray for people we can be very conscious of our own deficiencies and so we like to say, "in the name of Jesus" really forcefully. We know we are powerless in ourselves and so we raise our voice a little, seeking to be a little more assertive in our prayer. But the power to heal is not in our prayer; the power to heal is in the name of Jesus. This is no magical incantation. It is understanding that embodied in that one Name is the power of heaven and when we use it, we should expect things to happen! God has given us permission to use His name and when we do, all of heaven is listening.

In the book of Acts we read of the many healings and miracles that took place in the name of Jesus. There is a wonderful example of this in the third chapter. Here, we find a crippled man begging at the Beautiful Gate and, as Peter and John walk by, he asks them for money. The Bible says,

"Peter directed his gaze at him, as did John, and said, 'Look at us.' And he fixed his attention on them, expecting to receive something from them. But Peter said, 'I have no silver and gold, but what I do have I give to you. In the name of Jesus Christ of Nazareth, rise up and walk!' And he took him by the right hand and raised him up, and immediately his feet and ankles were made strong." (Acts 3:4-7 ESV)

This is the gospel of today. It is not just the gospel of the first century, but it is the dynamic power of Jesus. I can almost hear many saying at this point, "Well, if that's the case why aren't we seeing more lame people walking today and more answers to our prayers?" The frustrating thing is that we know God's kingdom has already come, but we have to realise that it has yet to come in all its fullness. As agents of this kingdom we have to learn to take a step forward every day. We are born into it through salvation and as we learn to pray and speak in the name of Jesus, we make slow but certain progress.

In certain nations of the world, this is happening in wonderful and astonishing ways, but it seems to be painfully slow for our westernised, sceptical and secular mindset. We need to press through the unbelief and declare that there is power in the name of Jesus and there is much more yet to be seen and experienced of the goodness of God around us. A chilling passage in the gospel of Matthew warns us of the power of unbelief:

"And when Jesus had finished these parables, He went away from there, and coming to His hometown He taught them in their synagogue, so that they were astonished, and said, 'Where did this man get this wisdom and these mighty works? Is not this the carpenter's son? Is not His mother called Mary? And are not His brothers James and Joseph and Simon and Judas? And are not all His sisters with us? Where then did this man get all these things?' And they took offense at Him. But Jesus said to them, 'A prophet is not without honour except in His hometown and in His own household.' And He did not do many mighty works there, because of their unbelief." (Matthew 13:53-58 ESV)

The power of unbelief was so strong in this town that even Jesus, the Son of God, could not perform many miracles. Let us not allow our cynicism and small worldview keep us from experiencing the kingdom of God in all its fullness.

It is not only miracles in the name of Jesus that are dynamic. When we are baptised in His name we are filled with His dynamic Holy Spirit. In Acts, Luke writes,

"And it happened that while Apollos was at Corinth, Paul passed through the inland country and came to Ephesus. There he found some disciples. And he said to them, 'Did you receive the Holy Spirit when you believed?' And they said, 'No, we have not even heard that there is a Holy Spirit.' And he said, 'Into what then were you baptized?' They said, 'Into John's baptism.' And Paul said, 'John baptized with the baptism of repentance, telling the people to believe in the one who was to come after him, that is, Jesus.' On hearing this, they were baptized in the name of the Lord Jesus. And when Paul had laid his hands on them, the Holy Spirit came on them, and they began speaking in tongues and prophesying." (Acts 19:1-6 ESV)

This is the full gospel! We repent of our sin, are baptised in water and we are filled with the Holy Spirit. This is the dynamic of the power of the name of Jesus.

In the process there may well also be deliverance from demonic bondage when the name of Jesus is spoken. Luke tells the story of the disciples returning from a mission. He writes,

"The seventy-two returned with joy, saying, 'Lord, even the demons are subject to us in your name!'" (Luke10:17 ESV)

I think that they were as surprised as you and I would be. They returned to Jesus saying, "It works!" I want to say with them, "It works!" I have been in many situations where I have seen people delivered from demonic powers in the name of Jesus. It is the most wonderful thing! If we have confidence in the name of Jesus then no weapon formed against us can prosper and we can speak to demonic forces and see them banished. I often feel that I have more faith to speak to demons than I do to sickness because in the Bible it is very clear. Demonic forces are not intended in God's creation and therefore they need to be expelled. They need expelling from buildings and they need expelling from people. In the name of Jesus, everyone can be set free from any oppressive demonic spirit when they want to be.

The Bible also encourages us to pray in the name of Jesus. Sometimes, our prayers seem weak and ineffective, but if, when we pray, we understand that we are praying in the name of Jesus, then we will know we are connecting with a dynamic name that will bring change. Jesus told His disciple at the last supper,

"Truly, truly, I say to you, whoever believes in Me will also do the works that I do; and greater works than these will he do, because I am going to the Father. Whatever you ask in My name, this I will do, that the Father may be glorified in the Son. If you ask me anything in My name, I will do it." (John.14:12-14 ESV)

Jesus also said,

"You did not choose me, but I chose you and appointed you that you should go and bear fruit and that your fruit should abide, so that whatever you ask the Father in My name, He may give it to you." (John15:16 ESV)

And,

"Truly, truly, I say to you, whatever you ask of the Father in My name, He will give it to you. Until now you have asked nothing in my name. Ask, and you will receive, that your joy may be full." (John16:23-24 ESV)

I want to encourage you to use that name more and more. We understand and are aware of our own weakness, but we also have to understand and acknowledge His great strength. I love the great verse in Paul's letter to the Colossians which says,

"Whatever you do, in word or deed, do everything in the name of the Lord Jesus, giving thanks to God the Father through Him." (Colossians 3:17 ESV)

Every day life should be done in the name of Jesus.

The highest Name

It is a wonderful privilege to be a follower of Jesus Christ, the One who has the highest name of all. We are in the best team that has ever walked the face of the earth. We are disciples of Jesus Christ, the King of kings and the Lord of lords, and the wonderful name of Jesus is higher and far more powerful than any other name that has ever or will ever exist.

The name of Jesus is always fresh, always full of power and never, ever, mediocre. However, at times, we can become over-familiar with the use of it. We sing countless songs about Him in our worship and read many books for our own study. Neither of these is wrong, of course, but they can detract from the simplicity of the word "Jesus" and the weight that is carried within it. Sometimes, just saying His name is enough.

Paul records for us that because of His incarnation, sufferings and death,

"...God has highly exalted Him and bestowed on Him the name that is above every name, so that at the name of Jesus every knee should bow, in heaven and on earth and under the earth, and every tongue confess that Jesus Christ is Lord, to the glory of God the Father.' (Philippians 2:9-11 ESV)

When Paul says, "therefore God exalted him" it literally means "super exalted." In other words, there is no higher place to go, there's no promotion higher – it is the super-exalted Jesus who has been given the highest place. Everything He laid down is now restored with much more. This man, Jesus, whom the angels said would come to save His people from their sins, is the same Jesus who was resurrected from the dead, ascended to the right hand of the Father and is glorified forevermore. Jesus has the highest Name.

There will come a day when He will be universally acknowledged by everyone on the earth. Whether people want to or not, they will be made to acknowledge that Jesus Christ is the exalted Son of God. Furthermore, there will be a universal confession that He is the Lord of heaven and earth. All will bow the knee.

This Jesus is now the resurrected, ascended and glorified Lord, the designated means by which God the Father reconciles all things to Himself through His suffering on the cross. What a Saviour!

Reflect and pray...

In the busyness of life with so many demands on my time, I will remember today that the name "Jesus" is higher than everything.

Lord, as I speak out your beautiful name, Jesus, I want to acknowledge that it has the power to calm me, soothe me, heal me, inspire me, unlock me, save me, comfort me and encourage me. I want to thank you for your name – that you are a Saviour, Friend and Brother. I will follow your example and in faith, reach out for your promise that by your Holy Spirit I will do greater things than you did. I promise to always honour you and give you the glory for all you do through me. Amen.

8

The Lord Who Sanctifies Me

In the Old Testament, two of the names of God appear to be woven together in two different Scriptures. The first is YAHWEH QADESH – the Lord who Sanctifies and the second is YAHWEH TSIDKENU – the Lord is our Righteousness.

A holy God

In Leviticus 20:8 God instructs the people of Israel to,

"Keep my statutes and do them; I am the Lord who sanctifies you." (ESV)

In another translation it reads,

"I am the Lord, who makes you holy." (NIV)

If you were looking to read a book of the Bible, it is likely you would not choose Leviticus, as it mainly contains detailed accounts of God's required rituals for His people, most of which are not relevant to 21st century life. But for the ancient Israelites, it was very important indeed. Eugene Peterson writes that Leviticus is,

"A narrative pause in the story of our ancestors ... an extended time-out of instruction, a detailed and meticulous preparation for living 'holy' in a culture that [did not] have the faintest idea what 'holy' [was]."

One of the most important things about this book is that it placed an emphasis on the fact that God was holy and the Israelites were not. His people had fallen into deep spiritual darkness, wandering far from grace and into moral depravity, and God was calling them back to a life of holiness that echoed His name YAHWEH QADESH – the Lord who sanctifies.

The extent of the moral decline was shocking. The Israelites had begun to align themselves to the Canaanite god Molech, sacrificing their children as appeasement. According to Keil and Delitzsch, Molech was,

"...represented by a [bronze] statue, which was hollow and capable of being heated, and formed with a bull's head, and arms stretched out to receive the children to be sacrificed."

God strongly condemned the practice of child sacrifice saying,

"You shall not give any of your children to offer them to Molech, and so profane the name of your God: I am the Lord." (Leviticus 18:21 ESV)

It is difficult to imagine how God's people could have stooped so low as to kill their own children on the altar of a foreign god, and yet here they were, sinking into sin at its blackest. Into this bleak picture came the revelation of the name of God, resplendent in holiness. God was angry, but He was also determined to lead His people away from their evil practices and idolatry back into relationship with Him.

Not only was there child sacrifice, but the Israelites had turned to occult practices and spiritualism. God would not tolerate this and expressed it thus:

"If a person turns to mediums and necromancers, whoring after them, I will set my face against that person and will cut him off from among his people." (Leviticus 20:6 ESV)

Our holiness does not depend upon our own effort, but upon God who is the one who sanctifies. Into our lives of sin and darkness He shines His light, challenging us to turn to face it and away from evil, leading us into a right relationship with Him. As with the Israelites, He does not want us to give way to idolatry or false teaching and practices. He is the source of everything and all we need for life in all its fullness. The Bible makes it very clear that,

"All have sinned and fall short of the glory of God." (Romans 3:23 ESV)

This should be liberating news for us, because in our quest for holiness we need to realise that holiness cannot be earned by hard work, by giving heavily to charities, or even attending more church meetings. Holiness is who God is and what God has declared over us.

Moving into the New Testament we find that, together with God, we are involved in the process of sanctification – of being made holy.

The apostle Paul prayed,

"Now may the God of peace himself sanctify you completely, and may your whole spirit and soul and body be kept blameless at the coming of our Lord Jesus Christ." (1 Thessalonians 5:23 ESV)

And to the church in Philippi, he wrote,

"...for it is God who works in you, both to will and to work for his good pleasure." (Philippians 2:13 ESV)

Just as Jesus is the example to us of holiness, making our sanctification possible by dying on the cross (Hebrews 12:2; 1 Peter 2:21; 1 John 2:6) so the Holy Spirit works within us to bring about the changes.

"The fruit of the Spirit is love, joy, peace, patience, kindness, goodness, faithfulness, gentleness, self-control; against such things there is no law." (Galatians 5:22-23 ESV)

In this process we quickly realise that our own attempts to cleanse ourselves and to mature in grace are futile in our own strength and efforts. Jesus, talking about spiritual fruit, said quite firmly,

"As the branch cannot bear fruit by itself, unless it abides in the vine, neither can you, unless you abide in Me. I am the vine; you are the branches. Whoever abides in Me and I in him, he it is that bears much fruit, for apart from Me you can do nothing." (John 15:4-5 ESV)

If we are to yield to the work of the Holy Spirit, this process requires us to participate and cooperate with God as we allow Him to change us. The Bible tells us that we are to present our bodies as a living sacrifice (Romans 12:1), giving God permission to work. To the Roman believers, Paul wrote,

"For if you live according to the flesh you will die, but if by the Spirit you put to death the deeds of the body, you will live." (Romans 8:13 ESV)

He also told the Philippians that it is,

"God who works in you, both to will and to work for His good pleasure." (Philippians 2:13 ESV)

It is for the "good pleasure" of a good God that we are to focus on the pursuit of holiness. Whilst we cannot make ourselves holy (only God can do that), we are told to abstain from sinful behaviour including immorality and youthful lusts. Choosing to reject sin and pursue a life after God leaves room for the Holy Spirit to come and cleanse, heal and sanctify us. Eugene Peterson talks about "no" being God's freedom word. He writes,

"Following Jesus means not following your impulses and appetites and whims and dreams, all of which are sufficiently damaged by sin to make them unreliable guides for getting any place worth going."

He adds,

"Only humans can say 'No'. Animals can't say 'No'. Animals do what instinct dictates. 'No' is a freedom word. I don't have to do what either my glands or my culture tells me to do."

We are to pursue righteousness (2 Timothy 2:22). Paul also writes,

"Therefore, if anyone cleanses himself from what is dishonourable, he will be a vessel for honourable use, set apart as holy, useful to the master of the house, ready for every good work." (2 Timothy 2:21 CEV)

When we say that God is "holy" it means that He is utterly and totally pure in every respect and is of a very different order to humanity. The word "holy" (Qodesh) is defined as "apartness, holiness, sacredness, separateness". Whilst it is true that God created mankind in His own image, it is only He who is holy.

In Leviticus 20:7-8 we read,

"Consecrate yourselves, therefore, and be holy, for I am the Lord your God. Keep My statutes and do them; I am the Lord who sanctifies you." (ESV)

This is YAHWEH QADESH – the Lord who Sanctifies. Sanctification does not happen quickly. God takes time with us. He works with the choices that we make to allow Him to change us to be more like Him and is patient with us if we prefer to explore in other directions at times. He is always committed to making us holy so that our lives become how they were intended to be when we were made in His image.

The holiness of God is breathtaking. In fact, we would not be able to stand in His presence if we encountered the fullness of it. The book of Isaiah gives us a glimpse in these verses from chapter 6:

"In the year that King Uzziah died I saw the Lord sitting upon a throne, high and lifted up; and the train of His robe filled the temple. Above Him stood the seraphim. Each had six wings: with two He covered his face, and with two He covered His feet, and with two He flew. And one called to another and said: 'Holy, holy, holy is the Lord of hosts; the whole earth is full of His glory!' And the foundations of the thresholds shook at the voice of Him who called, and the house was filled with smoke. And I said: 'Woe is me! For I am lost; for I am a man of unclean lips, and I dwell in the midst of a people of unclean lips; for my eyes have seen the King, the Lord of hosts!'" (Isaiah 6:1-5 ESV)

What a powerful image! At the end of the Bible, in the book of Revelation, there is virtually the same passage:

"And the four living creatures, each of them with six wings, are full of eyes all around and within, and day and night they never cease to say, 'Holy, holy, holy, is the Lord God Almighty, who was and is and is to come!'" (Revelation 4:8 ESV)

The complete and absolute holiness of God is central to our understanding of who He is as revealed in His name YAHWEH QADESH.

A righteous God

The second passage I want to examine is Jeremiah 23:5-6:

"'Behold, the days are coming,' declares the LORD, 'when I will raise up for David a righteous Branch, and He shall reign as King and deal wisely, and shall execute justice and righteousness in the land. In His days Judah will be saved, and Israel will dwell securely. And this is the name by which He will be called: "The Lord is our Righteousness."'" (ESV)

This name of God is YAHWEH TSIDKENU – the Lord is our Righteousness.

During this time the leaders of the nation of Israel had once again fallen away from God's design and desire to make them great by refusing to follow His statutes. They had become proud and ambitious, ignoring the shepherd heart of God in favour of harshness, selfishness and corruption. Instead of gathering and caring for the flock, the leaders were actually in the process of destroying and scattering them. We read,

"'Woe to the shepherds who destroy and scatter the sheep of My pasture!' declares the Lord. Therefore thus says the Lord, the God of

Israel, concerning the shepherds who care for my people: 'You have scattered my flock and have driven them away, and you have not attended to them.'" (Jeremiah 23:1-2 ESV)

God had given a mandate to Israel's leaders to lead with integrity, righteousness, truth and compassion. But the reality was that they were insecure, destructive and divisive. Everything was a mess and for this covenant people things looked very bleak indeed.

Into this dark place God promised to intervene to bring His light by providing a man who would truly be a Godly Shepherd. He would be no ordinary man – this was to be the promised Messiah, a branch from the line of David. His name was to be called YAHWEH TSIDKENU – the Lord is our Righteousness. He would be the Good Shepherd, the Great Shepherd, the Chief Shepherd: the one who would lead in the manner that God had intended.

God is committed to providing good leadership to His people and good leadership for His people. He is, of course, the ultimate Leader – holy in all His ways, loving, faithful and just – and He generously gives all of His leadership resources to those given responsibility to lead His people. We cannot be the leaders we should be in God without the infilling of His righteous Holy Spirit which sanctifies.

You may expect that this Scripture would say, "The Lord is righteous" and that would not be untrue. We know that there would be one who would come who would be righteous: Jesus. He would do everything the Father commanded and He would be pure in every way. However, this is not what this revelatory name means in the verses in Jeremiah. This name is YAHWEH TSIDKENU – the Lord is our Righteousness. Think about this for a while: it is not just that the Lord is righteous in Himself, but He is our Righteousness. In other words, our standing with God has nothing at all to do with our own goodness or righteousness, but with His! It is He who makes us righteous and

He who makes us holy.

People have struggled with this concept for centuries. They have felt that it was entirely their responsibility to make themselves holy and, feeling that they are unable to separate themselves from the world, they have entered communes or monastic orders only to find that they have taken their unsanctified human nature with them. Many have afflicted themselves with rods and scourges and have sought to beat holiness into themselves by punishing and subduing their physical bodies. Authentic holiness is never to do with legalism with all its rules and regulations – it is all about what God has said about us. It is a matter of faith in the finished work of Jesus.

In 1 Corinthians1: 30-31 we read,

"And because of Him you are in Christ Jesus, who became to us wisdom from God, righteousness and sanctification and redemption, so that, as it is written, 'Let the one who boasts, boast in the Lord.'" (ESV)

From the beginning of creation, God had purposed that we would be holy in His presence, not as a result of our own works, but because of the finished work of Jesus, the spotless Lamb of God. It is through His death on the cross that we are made righteous. We would never have been able to do that ourselves, so we need to relinquish the fleshly ways of self-righteousness and choose to trust in God's.

I have chosen to interweave the names YAHWEH QADESH – the Lord who Sanctifies and YAHWEH TSIDKENU – the Lord is our Righteousness because It is my view that these two names of God are mutually compatible. God has destined us for holiness – that is His plan for our lives and He desires that we live rightly before Him in purity of heart. When we remember just how corrupt mankind can get and how corrupt leadership can become, it is vital that we set our focus on His ultimate goodness.

At times, however, we can find this difficult to believe. We tend to measure ourselves against others who seem to be more holy than we are and we can feel inferior or anxious that we will never "get there".

Let me tell you about a slave trafficker named John Newton. Newton was born in 1725 and grew up to become a captain of a ship which transported slaves. He was a drunkard and a gambler; he swore profusely and was intensely disliked by his crew. In the middle of a severe storm off the coast of Donegal, he called out to God telling Him that if he was delivered from the waves, he would dedicate his life to serving Him.

Miraculously, Newton survived and, true to his word, he gave his life to Jesus, asking forgiveness for all the wrong things he had done over the years. His deep gratitude to God flowed out through the words of his hymn "Amazing Grace", which he penned some years after his conversion and which is still a favourite today:

Amazing Grace, how sweet the sound
That saved a wretch like me.
I once was lost but now am found
Was blind but now I see.

Newton had declared himself to be a wretch, which was exactly what he had become. Morally, he was at the bottom of the pile, but it was precisely there that he found the sweet forgiveness that God gives through Christ. By a simple prayer he was cleansed and made righteous. It was grace, not works, that saved him.

The apostle Paul wrote,

"For by grace you have been saved through faith. And this is not your own doing; it is the gift of God, not a result of works, so that no one may boast." (Ephesians 2:8-9 ESV)

There are many people who feel that they are not as bad as a John Newton and so will not be in need of the same grace. In the Western world especially, it is easy to feel that we are actually doing alright as we surround ourselves with "good choices" and take time to build a decent life. We may not murder, steal or traffic slaves, but the Bible is very clear that being decent will not get us into heaven. Decency is not the same as holiness. Even the apostle Paul, who had a very impressive religious pedigree, described himself as the chief of sinners. At one point in his life he felt that his religious pedigree and achievements stood him in good stead with God, until he met with Jesus. At that point all of his own righteousness became nothing but a bunch of dirty rags.

Neither is being raised in a Christian home a recipe for holiness. In my own experience of growing up I did not have much opportunity to sin at all. For one thing, my father would not let me and also I was at church meetings all the time! I think the worst thing I ever did was take an aspirin!

John Wesley, the founder of the Methodist Movement, was studying at Oxford when he developed a very strict regime in order to find God. He would get up very early in the morning to read the Scriptures in their original language. He would study hard and would fast on a weekly basis. Gradually, Wesley began to meet with other like-minded people and in their quest for holiness they would seek out the poor to help them, giving time and money to meet their needs. People around them thought this behaviour was ridiculous and the little group were to become known derisively as "The holy club".

Recently I read about George Whitfield who became involved in the Great Awakening in America and who also studied at Oxford. Before he became a Christian he would steer clear of the Wesley brothers because he also viewed them as weird and strange. There is a quaint story of how Whitfield, who earnestly desired to meet and talk to Charles Wesley, would pace up and down the corridor housing Wesley's room, waiting for there to be no one around before he knocked on the door. He really did not want to be seen to be associating with them, despite being curious about their methods of pursuing God.

There is no doubt that Wesley and his friends desired and sought to live holy lives, but in all their efforts they were missing the fact that Jesus had actually paid for all their sins and all they had to do was trust Him. They thought that if they gave and served and toiled that they would eventually become holy and earn acceptance with God. John Wesley even served as a missionary in America, seeking to progress into more holiness.

It was some time after in London, where he had returned depressed and feeling an abject failure, that he ended up in a meeting where he heard a reading of Martin Luther's preface to Paul's letter to the Romans. It was there that the penny dropped and, in his own words, "I felt my heart strangely warmed." He realised that salvation could not come through any religious achievement, but by simply trusting in the finished work of Jesus on the cross. He had a key revelation: it is God who makes us holy and righteous.

When Jesus was crucified, a thief turned to Him in penitence, asking to be remembered by the Lord when He came into His kingdom. At that very moment Jesus said to him,

"Truly, I say to you, today you will be with me in Paradise." (Luke 23:43 ESV)

The thief launched all his faith towards Christ and found instant forgiveness. This is so encouraging for us today. We know that whatever our background, history or misdemeanours, by simply by turning to

Christ we can find forgiveness.

When we compare ourselves with others it is easy to become riddled with unnecessary guilt. Maybe you imagine a great auditorium in heaven where the most holy of people have the front seats and you are actually in the car park outside peering in.

The picture is wrong because the one who is our righteousness actually stands with us covering us with His own righteousness. God is on our case to sanctify us, to change and reshape us, which requires that we daily yield to His work in us.

Positional righteousness

There are three aspects to righteousness. The first is positional righteousness. This refers to the fact that the moment we turn to God in repentance, seeking forgiveness, it is given to us because Jesus has become our substitute, meaning that we receive a full pardon. From that point our position has changed. The Bible tells us that the guilty sinner is transformed from darkness to light:

"He has delivered us from the domain of darkness and transferred us to the kingdom of His beloved Son." (Colossians 1:13 ESV)

Practical righteousness

This is where our lives begin to change and we begin to make a difference here on the earth. It is what happens as we submit ourselves to the God who makes us holy, meaning that we can begin to become good news in our community. Our language and thought patterns change as God starts His work in us and instead of pleasing others and ourselves, we start to want to please God.

Process righteousness

This aspect of righteousness can easily be missed, especially by those of us of a charismatic persuasion. In this process we commit ourselves to God on a daily basis and we are gradually changed into the likeness of Christ. Then throughout our journey with Christ we become very different people at the end of our earthly life from who we were as we accepted Christ.

How does this work practically in our lives? If it is true that God is YAHWEH QADESH – the Lord who Sanctifies and YAHWEH TSIDKENU – the Lord is our Righteousness, are there things that He has put in place to make the process work? I believe there are and so I want to suggest the following:

The blood of Christ

God cleanses us by the blood of His Son, Jesus Christ. The writer to the Hebrews wrote,

"Jesus also suffered outside the gate in order to sanctify the people through His own blood." (Hebrews 13:12 ESV)

The blood of Jesus brings us near to God and gives us confidence to approach Him (see Ephesians 2:19 and Hebrews 10:19). The aged apostle John wrote that,

"If we walk in the light, as He is in the light, we have fellowship with one another, and the blood of Jesus his Son cleanses us from all sin." (1 John 1:7 ESV)

A beautiful old hymn says, "What can wash away my sin? Nothing but the blood of Jesus…" When we sin and fail, we can come to Him to be washed completely clean.

The discipline of God

The Bible tells that God disciplines those whom He loves. The writer of Hebrews says,

"My son, do not regard lightly the discipline of the Lord, nor be weary when reproved by Him. For the Lord disciplines the one He loves, and chastises every son whom He receives." (Hebrews12: 5-6 ESV)

Discipline is not always easy to take. The writer to the Hebrews continues,

"…for the moment all discipline seems painful rather than pleasant, but later it yields the peaceful fruit of righteousness to those who have been trained by it." (Hebrews 12:11 ESV)

Discipline involves God changing us and shaping us to make us more like Him. He teaches us to trust Him, whatever the circumstances that surround us, in good and bad times. In fact, our response to adverse circumstances will often determine our levels of holiness. He looks to see how we react when things go wrong and He also watches to see if we will be thankful when things go right.

William Carey was known as "the father of modern missions" and he mainly ministered to the continent of India where he saw remarkable success. Preceding the success, however, were seven years where nothing happened at all. A good number of us, if placed in similar circumstances would feel that our faith was non-existent and we would become very discouraged, probably at that point ready to pack up and go home. Carey, however, recognised that he was being led through a process where God was disciplining him. It was a very difficult time, mainly because his wife suffered a complete mental breakdown and was hospitalised, unable to communicate with him at all. On top of that, his first son died of dysentery. Nevertheless, Carey pressed through those tough times because he realised that God was using these hardships to shape him into the man for the task set before him. Carey went on to plant many churches and was a major influence for the gospel in India.

These things are profound and it is a challenge to us to learn to trust God in the dark seasons of our lives. He is committed to making us holy by all means and He will bring us through such times, shaping us and forming us into the men and women that he can easily use.

The Word of God

When we read the Bible it purifies our minds and cleanses our souls. Jesus says to His disciples,

"Already you are clean because of the word that I have spoken to you." (John 15:3 ESV)

He then prayed to his Father,

"Sanctify them in the truth; your word is truth." (John 17:17 ESV)

We are cleansed and sanctified by the Word of God.

The Spirit of God

God also works in our lives by the Holy Spirit. When we look back into the Old Testament we see that much of the spiritual life of Israel was regulated by Levitical rules and observances. Any visitation of the Spirit was a rare occurrence and it all served to point to the future when the Spirit would be poured out plentifully on the day of Pentecost. Today and every day the Holy Spirit empowers us to live the Christian life in all its fullness. He lives within us and as we co-operate with Him and yield to Him, the fruit of the Spirit grows and begins to show. This fruit actually is the manifestation of the life of Christ. Paul writes,

"The fruit of the Spirit is love, joy, peace, patience, kindness, goodness, faithfulness, gentleness, self-control; against such things there is no law." (Galatians 5:22-23 ESV)

Paul also wrote about being sanctified by the Spirit:

"But on some points I have written to you very boldly by way of reminder, because of the grace given me by God to be a minister of Christ Jesus to the Gentiles in the priestly service of the gospel of God, so that the offering of the Gentiles may be acceptable, sanctified by the Holy Spirit." (Romans 15:15-16 ESV)

The Holy Spirit wants to walk daily with us so that He can guide us and lead us. He wants to be our heavenly companion, leading us into the pure ways and clean thoughts of God.

This is not a passive growing into holiness where God does all the work and we simply get on with life. Rather, it is a submitting to His way of doing things and co-operating with Him. The late Judson Cornwall once gave the illustration of a large ship coming into port. As it approaches, the captain of the ship requests the services of the harbour pilot who knows the waters of the port intimately. He knows what to avoid, he knows where all the sandbanks are and he knows how to manoeuvre a large ship into its mooring. It is not the pilot who takes over the wheel, however. That responsibility belongs to the captain. The captain actually steers the boat while the pilot stands just behind him, talking to him, telling him what to avoid, what power level the engines should be running at and, in fact, telling him every detail that he needs to know in order to bring the ship safely into port. All the time it is the captain who has to decide whether to yield to the directions of the pilot or not.

The Holy Spirit was not just given for a one-off experience after Jesus ascended into heaven. He is with us today and every day. He is our comforter, our guide, a loving presence; He is the pilot for the journey into harbour. As we progress through life with Him, His fruit also grows within us and each day we become a little more like Him. There will come a day when we shall see the Lord for who He is and we have the promise that we shall be like Him. Isn't that wonderful?

Coming home

In conclusion, I want to recount a story I read in one of Philip Yancey's books, about God's forgiveness and kindness.

A young girl aged around 14 or 15 years of age, living in the United States, one day had a massive argument with her parents and she told them that she was leaving home. There had been a history of tension in the home and she had had enough. She packed her bags and took a greyhound coach on a long journey to Detroit. She had picked a big city as she wanted to distance herself as much as she could from her home.

After some days of being cold and hungry, wondering whether she had made the right decision, she walked into a shopping centre and sat against a vent blowing out warm air. While she was there she started thinking about the decision she had made and whether she ought to consider going home again, but decided that her parents probably would not want to receive her back into the house. Suddenly, a very smartly dressed man came up to her and offered to help. She began to tell him her story and he told her that he could easily find her somewhere to live and could also get her a job. She got up and accompanied him to his car and then he told her that he could easily provide for her but there were a few things that he would require from her in return.

Soon, she found herself in a large house with other young girls. True to his word, this smart gentleman, who was the landlord of the property, gave her somewhere to stay and food to eat, but he also introduced her into the dark world of child prostitution. Before long, she was fully involved in the trade and feeling riddled with shame.

As she existed in this twilight world, grieving for her past, she often thought about her parents back home, wondering if they would ever welcome her back again. A year passed during which she had been very active in the prostitution trade, eventually becoming quite ill, often vomiting violently. The landlord came to see her and threw her out of the house because, in his view, she had become useless to him. She was back on the streets and she began to think of her home again, finally deciding to pluck up the courage to ring her parents. She wanted to know if they loved her enough to allow her to return. If they didn't, then she would have to think of something else. She made the call and found that there was no one home, so she left a message on the answering machine.

She said something like, "Mum and Dad, I've made a mess of my life, I've got myself into deep trouble, but I want an opportunity to come home. This is what I'm going to do – I'm going to get on a Greyhound bus and I am going to come home to the depot in the city. I'll be there at midnight tomorrow night and if you get this message and if you really want me to come home, please be there to greet me. If you're not there, and I'd understand it if you're not, I'll get back on the bus and I'll go to another destination and I'll have to live with the life that I have chosen."

Since she had to leave a message on an answering machine, she had no idea as to whether it had been received. She got on the bus the next day, however, and travelled the long journey home, reaching the depot around midnight. Everything was in darkness and she felt an intense sadness in the pit of her stomach. She thought to herself, "No one is here." Getting off the bus, she approached the door of the depot and as she tentatively pushed open the door, suddenly the lights came on and party poppers exploded. She stood there stunned as she saw about thirty people standing there. Her grandfather and grandmother, her parents, her friends were all there. Her father pushed his way through the small crowd, hugged her and said, "Welcome home!"

This true story beautifully illustrates the welcoming love of God our Father. It is not complicated. It has nothing to do with our frenetic attempts to find Him; it is all about a Heavenly Father who comes running towards us, welcoming us back home. Like the story of the prodigal son, He wants to put a ring on our finger, wrap us in the finest linen and throw a party. It is all made possible because of what Jesus has done. He is our righteousness and He is our sanctification and all we need to do is respond to His wonderful invitation. He is the Good Shepherd who wants to lead us, not push us, into all that He has completed for us and He has a wonderful inheritance waiting for us to walk into.

Reflect and pray...

No matter how hard I try, I cannot make myself holy and righteous. Only God can do that.

Lord, I am tired of trying to make myself good. I know that I cannot change myself deep down without surrendering to the beautiful work of your Holy Spirit, who knows exactly what I need for a life of holiness and righteousness. I understand the difference between self-righteousness and your righteousness and today I choose you! Thank you for Jesus who has sanctified me by dying in my place. Lord, teach me to yield to you day by day and help me to celebrate as I see the fruit of your Spirit growing in my life, making me more and more like you. Amen.

9

The Lord is my Banner

Within the Bible, particularly in the Old Testament, there are many accounts of raging battles and fierce wars, more often than not involving the Israelites and sometimes as a result of God's intervention or direction. For many who have read the stories over the centuries, the concept of so much bloodshed and aggression is a difficult one and it can be a challenge to explain it in the light of a God who is loving and good. We can try to see it through the filter of the Fall in Genesis and the choices of Adam and Eve, but I do not want to dwell on it here as I prefer to focus on the good news of how God set in motion a restoration programme to draw everything and everyone back under His Lordship (see Ephesians 1:10; Philippians 2:10 and Colossians 1:19). As He did so, strife and conflict would be inevitable, and so one of His names from early in the Old Testament, as revealed to the Israelites for their encouragement, was YAHWEH NISSI – the Lord is my Banner.

In Exodus 17:8-16 we read about how Amalek came to fight Israel. This warring tribe was directly descended from Esau and they had been a thorn in Israel's side for centuries. In this passage we see their first recorded head-on encounter with Israel and Moses appointed Joshua to lead the army and engage Amalek in battle. Moses, along with Aaron and Hur, climbed to the top of a hill to intercede for victory and when the battle was won, Moses built an altar to the Lord to commemorate it. The Scriptures say that,

"Moses built an altar and called the name of it, The Lord Is My Banner saying, 'A hand upon the throne of the Lord! The Lord will have war with Amalek from generation to generation.'" (Exodus 17:15-16 ESV)

The original Hebrew for "The Lord is my Banner" here is Yahweh Nissi.

This particular story brings home some truths that are pertinent to our lives today. It is an account not to be locked away in some historical filing cabinet, but to be read regularly and from which we can learn the strategy of the enemy in coming against the people of God and how God responds to it on their behalf. This story needs to touch our lives today and for that reason we are now going to look at it in some depth, as we draw towards the end of this book.

The story

"Then Amalek came and fought with Israel at Rephidim. So Moses said to Joshua, 'Choose for us men, and go out and fight with Amalek. Tomorrow I will stand on the top of the hill with the staff of God in my hand.' So Joshua did as Moses told him, and fought with Amalek, while Moses, Aaron, and Hur went up to the top of the hill. Whenever Moses held up his hand, Israel prevailed, and whenever he lowered his hand, Amalek prevailed. But Moses' hands grew weary, so they took a stone and put it under him, and he sat on it, while Aaron and Hur held up his hands, one on one side, and the other on the other side. So his hands were steady until the going down of the sun. And Joshua overwhelmed Amalek and his people with the sword. Then the Lord said to Moses, 'Write this as a memorial in a book and recite it in the ears of Joshua, that I will utterly blot out the memory of Amalek from under heaven.' And Moses built an altar and called the name of it, The Lord is my Banner, saying, 'A hand upon the throne of the Lord!

The Lord will have war with Amalek from generation to generation.'"
(Exodus 17:8-16 ESV)

The Amalekite tribe was descended from Amalek who was the son of
Eliphaz, the son of Esau, Jacob's brother. Esau was therefore Amalek's
grandfather. Amalek himself was born out of a relationship between
his father and a woman called Timna, one of Eliphaz's concubines,
making him a son of the flesh and not of the promise. In addition
to this, there was also something in the DNA of this line that was
violently aggressive towards Israel, and the story of that aggression
started in the heart of Esau when he sold his birthright to Jacob
in exchange for some stew in Genesis 25:29-34. Esau's desire for
immediate satisfaction usurped the promised blessing of God over
his life. In fact, the Scripture says that Esau "despised his birthright"
(Genesis 25:34 ESV).

Unfortunately, this had serious implications for the generations to
come. Amalek was raised from childhood with the legacy that piping
hot stew was more important than any lasting inheritance. In effect,
"Feed me" replaced "Lead me". The quest to satisfy the flesh replaced
the reverence for the deeper promise of a rich destiny.

In Deuteronomy 25:17-18, we see another glimpse of Amalek's
strategy:

"Remember what Amalek did to you on the way as you came out
of Egypt, how he attacked you on the way when you were faint and
weary, and cut off your tail, those who were lagging behind you, and he
did not fear God." (ESV)

The Amalekites did not engage in clean warfare. Rather, they picked
off the weak, weary and the vulnerable first in a cowardly attempt to
reduce numbers. They would periodically attack the people of God as

they journeyed through the wilderness out of Egypt. It was as they left the bondage they had been in for years that they were set upon. This is crucial for our understanding of how the enemy will try to ambush us on our walk with Jesus. The Israelites were not attacked while they lived in Egypt because they were already in bondage. As soon as they broke free form their enemy's control, that was when the trouble started. When we are under the enemy's power there are few problems, but as soon as we leave "Egypt" – a spiritual synonym for the world – that is when we face opposition and we come under spiritual attack. Effectively, we enter into a war-zone where we become the enemy's prime targets.

Over the years, I have seen many people publicly express their faith by being baptized. Sadly, of those who have done this, a large number no longer follow Christ. They went through the waters with all sincerity and seriousness, but they did not understand that in identifying themselves with Christ they became enemies of the darkness. Once we nail our colours to the mast and make the step to follow the Lord, the enemy has a well-developed strategy to trip us up, to distract us or to lead us away from the light. This is why, when the gospel is preached, the implications of following Christ must be made clear: it will cost us. Coming to and following after Christ can be the end of one set of problems and the beginning of others. The journey with the Lord is filled with joy and pain, mountain top experiences and valley experiences, good and not so good times. Sometimes it is a head-on battle and we are required to think about where we will focus our attention in the midst of it. If we lift our heads, we will see that "YAHWEH NISSI – the Lord is my Banner" is in the field of battle with us – and a far superior strategy than that of our enemy. We have to stay focused on Him and His ways, never relying on our own strength and strategies.

If we feel weak, tired of living the Christian life, vulnerable or fed up, it is important to lean into the one who is our strength. No battle that is waged against us, no strategy of the enemy to pick us off, is greater than the power of God which protects and shields us from danger. Make the choice to realign yourself today with the truth of who God is in times of attack. Keep in step with those around you who are journeying alongside you so you do not fall behind.

So now back to the battle itself in Exodus 17. This time, instead of a surprise ambush, it is a full frontal attack. Moses instructs Joshua to choose men to fight in the battle, whilst adopting a different strategy for himself. Accompanied by Aaron and Hur, Moses climbs to the top of the hill and there proceeds to intercede for Joshua and the army. As he lifts his arms and his staff in prayer, the Lord comes alongside Joshua and the troops, and Amalek is beaten back. After a while, however, his arms begin to tire and his staff begins to lower. At that point, Amalek fights back and makes progress. It is quite possible that Amalek noticed this lowering of the staff and took fresh courage, beginning the fight back.

There are two important observations to make here. The first is that leadership often fights the battles on behalf of the people from a different position and it is often their fight that wins the day. Moses installed Joshua as the main warrior on the ground, taking himself away from the physical frontline to cry out to God for victory. His decision to do this was crucial for the end result, even though it may have looked like he was abandoning the masses when they needed him the most. Moses understood that leadership is not always about being seen to be at the front; it is about engaging with the heart of God for the people. Sometimes this is visible, sometimes more hidden.

Secondly, Moses, like any other leader before or since, became tired and weary and needed Aaron and Hur to come alongside him. It does not take much wisdom to realise that we are not designed to battle on our own. Aaron and Hur join with Moses, making him sit down to take the weight off his arms. Our authority in the battle does not have to be demonstrative and noisy. It can be, and should be, restful and in the company of leaders who fully support us, even if it takes all day or longer. This posture of sitting and exercising authority is well documented in Scripture (see Psalm 110:1, Ephesians 1:20, Colossians 3:1 and Hebrews 10:12) True authority is restful authority, finding peace in the finished work of Christ.

In this passage, there are four additional aspects to consider:

The raised staff

Moses stood on the hill with a staff in his hand, which speaks of authority. Although the staff was just an ordinary piece of wood, God told Moses to use it as a symbol of His own authority. When we begin to familiarise ourselves with and use that which God has given us, then we will see kingdom authority at work. Ordinary men and women, using ordinary things that God has told them to pick up, can be mighty conquerors in His kingdom.

The lifted hands

Moses not only lifted the staff, he lifted his hands to the throne of God in intercession. Moses recognised that the power to win was not located within himself, or even with the army of Israel – it was located in the throne of God. He therefore physically reached high to access heavenly resources. In the same way we need to continue to reach into the heart of God for our breakthroughs.

The supportive friends

God intervened in Israel's battles, even to the extent of throwing large

stones down from heaven (Joshua 10:11) and sending the angel of the
Lord to take out 185,000 Assyrians (2 Kings 19:35). However, God
prefers to fight battles in partnership with His people. Even Jesus,
when He was praying agonised prayers in the garden of Gethsemane
wanted human friends with Him and not just angelic friends. I
believe that supportive ministry is as important as frontline ministry
and would go so far as to say that the latter falters badly without the
former. Every act needs a support act. It is vital that we give time to
build deep relationships with one another so we have the support we
need when the battles rage.

The declared name

When the battle was over, Moses built an altar and declared its name:
YAHWEH NISSI – the Lord is my Banner. For the Israelites, God
had been their banner, their flag and their ensign under whom they
had found victory. For us today, Christ is the Lamb who was sacrificed
on the altar, but that work needs to be strongly declared as, in so doing,
it releases more of His power and authority across the earth. In all of
our battles, the Lord wants us to look only to Him – the source of our
encouragement and strength. Under His banner and watchful eye we
will win great battles together.

Put on the armour!

Not many people fall away from following the Lord because of
theological difficulties or even strong demonic attacks. They usually
slide away because of unresolved issues in their lives that have been
ticking away and have never been brought under the Lordship of
Christ. They start watching certain programmes on television that are
not wholesome or helpful; they get involved with relationships that

are destructive; lines begin to be crossed and before they know it they stop reading the Bible and aligning their lives to God. They do not take seriously that there is a spiritual enemy who strongly desires to introduce neglect and damage into their spiritual lives.

I remember the day that I was baptized in the Holy Spirit. The event was so dramatic for me that I knew it was the end of my old way of living and the beginning of a new way of living. I found myself speaking in a language that I had never learned and I encountered a powerful, supernatural world where everything spiritual became more real to me. It was wonderful! But alongside all this, I also knew that the enemy of my soul was very real. Up to that point, I had lived so comfortably in the dimensions of this world that I did not notice my enemy. But now I was confronted with another dimension of life that was both wonderful and fearful. I knew I needed to look to YAHWEH NISSI for the rest of my life, as it would be only under His banner that I would be victorious.

The people of God have always been the target of aggression, oppression and violence. Both the Jewish nation and the Church of Christ over the centuries have suffered persecution and horrible atrocities. Paul says outright to Timothy that,

"…all who desire to live a godly life in Christ Jesus will be persecuted…" (2 Timothy 3:12 ESV)

All this tells us that there is a real presence of evil in this world that wants to destroy both everything God is doing and anyone who gets involved with what He is doing. Every move forward that God takes with His people is challenged and confronted by Satan, the enemy of our souls. This is the reality that we have to learn to live with. Winston Churchill once wrote, "If you don't have enemies in life you have never stood up for anything." Anyone who is seriously in love with Jesus and is manifesting the power of the risen Jesus in his life will eventually experience suffering. Moses, the great deliverer of Israel and Jesus, the Son of God, both suffered attempts on their lives while they were still infants. As we progress in our walk with the Lord we will soon discover the presence and the power of evil in and around us. We are in a battle zone. Satan fights dirty, unfairly and without mercy.

When we use this phrase, YAHWEH NISSI – the Lord is my Banner, we are not thinking about the banners with pictures and texts that we find in many of our churches. These are helpful and colourful, but they do not portray the fact that it is the Lord who is our banner. The word "banner" is Nês and means, "something lifted up, a standard, a signal, signal pole, ensign, banner, sign, sail". It is taken from the root Nâsas, which means, "to gleam from afar, that is, to be conspicuous as a signal; carrying the idea of a flag fluttering in the wind; a raised beacon". It is something to be looked at as a rallying point that gives heart and courage. In the story found in Numbers 21:8-9, Moses made a bronze serpent and fastened it to a pole so that all who had been bitten by snakes could look up to it and be healed. Jesus used this as an analogy when He said,

"And as Moses lifted up the serpent in the wilderness, so must the Son of Man be lifted up, that whoever believes in Him may have eternal life." (John 3:14-15 ESV)

So in one sense, just as the serpent on the pole was a rallying point for healing, so the cross of Christ was also like an ensign, a rallying point for healing, salvation and restoration. We look to His finished work and we are saved.

Many years ago, flag-bearers used to carry the colours of their regiment into battle to inspire the troops. In military thinking, the colours not only brought inspiration, they carried something of the battalion's honour and therefore they were to be defended at all costs. To lose their colours in battle was a great dishonour to any regiment or battalion. The colours on the pole were intrinsic to the morale of the troops.

The authentic Christian life will contain battles. The battles in the Old and New Testaments are there to instruct us for our own journey and it is important we take time to absorb their true meaning. We will be tested and tempted, as Jesus was; we will be assailed at times with sickness, doubts, fears and even dark thoughts.

When Paul writes to the believers in Ephesus about spiritual warfare he uses the language of Roman military armour (Ephesians 6:10-17). Using military language, he writes to Timothy saying,

"Share in suffering as a good soldier of Christ Jesus. No soldier gets entangled in civilian pursuits, since his aim is to please the one who enlisted him." (2 Timothy 2:3-4 ESV)

Paul writes to the church in Ephesus,

"Put on the whole armour of God, that you may be able to stand against the schemes of the devil." (Ephesians 6:11 ESV)

In the past, I used to think that if I kept my head down, did what was right and followed Jesus quietly, I would not be attacked. My experience over the years, however, tells me that it is not like that. As Christians, we cannot take our uniform off and just mingle with the crowd, pretending that we are not on God's side. When we commit our lives into the loving hands of our Father, we are trusting Him with every aspect of it. We can trust Him to look after us in the battles we will inevitably face, whatever we choose to do with our lives. It is true that some seasons of life feel like more of a battle than others and some people, by the nature of what they do for God, are more open to attack. But God never leaves our side, and will always provide us with the full armour we need to face our enemy.

So we do not need to fear: we just need to put it on!

Reflect and pray...

There is no battle I will face that Jesus has not experienced before me.

Lord, the Bible talks of you as a "Mighty Warrior" and I want to thank you today that you ride out to battle on my behalf. I know that your name covers me and protects me when I face circumstances that I do not understand. I know that my life is hidden in you and I am your child. You have given me everything I need to face my enemy head on and win, so I ask for your banner to cover me completely today and always so that I will not fear. Thank you for the people who journey with me, holding up my arms when I need it. I pray that you would equip me to do the same for those who find themselves weary and tired so that, together, we can walk in more and more victory in the days to come. Amen.

A Name For Every Situation in Life

Throughout this book we've examined some of the different names of God and through understanding them, I hope, have gained fresh perspectives and a deeper understanding of the nature and character of our Father. This has not been an exhaustive study, by any means, but I have wanted to focus particularly on what God desires to be for us in the circumstances of life.

One of the things that consistently struck me whilst looking into these revealed aspects of His character is that for every challenge we have in life, God has a name. But not only does He have a name, He embodies that name. In other words, for every need we are ever likely to have, God has an answer and that answer is Himself.

If we are troubled or stressed out by the pressures of life's circumstances, He is our Peace. He does not simply say to us in a passive sense, "Don't worry, everything will be alright....". Rather, He beckons us into His presence and there we find we are consumed by His peace - an active, living peace that transcends everything else in life.

When we are embattled and feeling crushed by oppression, He is our Banner - our Protector - the one who not only watches over us, but actively goes into battle on our behalf and fights our cause.

Above all, He is our Saviour - the one who has rescued us, such is His commitment to our eternal wellbeing. I encourage you to continue looking into the Name above all names and continue to discover all He wants to be and do for you.

About the Author

Stuart Bell is the Senior Pastor of New Life Church with multiple locations in the north of England. Stuart also heads up the Groundlevel network of 100+ churches.

He is actively involved in a number of national leadership forums and often ministers into South Africa and America. Stuart is an international speaker and teacher and has written a number of books. Stuart is married to Irene and they have three children and two grandsons.